ANXIETY HACKS

WORKBOOK

PROVEN TECHNIQUES, TOOLS AND TIPS TO CALMNESS

Kate Hudson-Hall, Dip. AdvHYP (NSHAP)

Anxiety Hacks Proven techniques, tools, and tips to calmness

The resources in this book are provided for informational purposes only and should not be used to replace the specialized training and professional judgment of a health care or mental health care professional.

ISBN: 978-1-7384630-0-8

THE ANXIETY HACKS
FREE BONUS COMPANION COURSE

Unlock an inspiring journey to conquer anxiety with the FREE Anxiety Hacks Bonus Companion Course.

Join me now for an immersive experience:

- Gain access to enlightening bonus video demonstrations for every technique.
- Enjoy exclusive content and valuable resources to amplify your progress.
- Dive into downloadable worksheets and templates tailored to each Hackster.

Step into the next chapter of your anxiety-free life – sign up today and empower yourself for lasting positive change!
See you on the other side!

Visit the following link to get free access to your bonus materials now:

https://anxietyhacks.info/info-step1/

DEDICATION

For those who dare believe they CAN change.

"Within the cocoon of anxiety,
find the gift to transform
into a butterfly
of bravery and strength."

Kate Hudson-Hall

CONTENTS

INTRODUCTION

"Imagine a butterfly elegantly sailing the breeze of change. Your thoughts can be wings steering you to new peaks" – Kate Hudson-Hall

Are you ready to take control of your life and free yourself from the suffocating grip of anxiety?

- I am excited to introduce you to the Anxiety Hacks Workbook. This is either a standalone workbook or the perfect companion to the widely acclaimed, best-selling, award-winning "***Anxiety Hacks: Proven Techniques, Tools and Tips to Calmness***."

The Anxiety Hacks Workbook is more than just pages: it's your roadmap to a life where anxiety takes a backseat. My mission? Equipping you with the tools, insights, and techniques for profound positive transformation.

As you flip through these super helpful pages, get ready to unravel anxiety's mysteries. We'll journey from understanding its triggers to mastering tools and techniques to usher in calmness. Each "hackster" is a stepping stone toward a version of you that is more in control, at ease, and relaxed.

But this isn't a read-and-forget deal. The magic unfolds when you step into the game. This workbook is your ticket to change, but only if you're ready to dive in. Effort, commitment, and a sprinkle of consistency – it's where the real magic happens.

Consider this workbook your secret weapon for feeling like the boss of your own brain. Inside is the power you need to rewrite your story with anxiety and build a life that's all about fulfillment and achievements.

My name is Kate Hudson-Hall, and I am your companion and therapist on this journey to conquer anxiety. As an anxiety therapist with 23 years of experience in the field, I've navigated the twists and turns of anxiety personally and professionally. I bring a blend of personal wisdom and professional expertise. Please think of me as your savvy navigator committed to steering you through anxiety's challenges toward a life filled with understanding and tranquility.

We are here to celebrate the small wins because each step forward is a victory. Picture it now: less anxiety and more calmness. It's not a mere possibility. It's the transformation awaiting you on the last page of this workbook.

So, let's dive into this journey, where every page propels you toward the life you have been dreaming of.

Here is how to use this workbook and why it's the most powerful tool at your disposal.

HOW TO USE THIS WORKBOOK:

What do you call a chapter in an Anxiety Hacks book? A Hackster! Well, that is what I call them.

So, there are 7 Hacksters to work through to take yourself from feeling anxious to learning the techniques, tools, and tips to calm your anxiety.

To maximize the benefits of using this workbook, you have two options:

- **A Dynamic Duo:** Whether you've already delved into "Anxiety Hacks "or not, this workbook is designed to be your loyal partner. Use it with the book for a comprehensive and deeply transformative experience. If you haven't acquired your copy of "***Anxiety Hacks***" yet, grab it now to supercharge your anxiety-busting journey https://www.bklnk.com/B0BLVPSV67

- **Standalone Strength:** If you're looking for a powerful resource to conquer anxiety, the "***Anxiety Hacks Workbook***" is a self-contained treasure trove of exercises, tables, techniques, and insights. It's your one-stop solution for dismantling anxiety habits and behavior patterns.

Deep Exploration: I would encourage you to embark on this journey with dedication. Complete each exercise meticulously. The devil is in the details. The more you invest in each exercise, the more you'll reap in terms of:

  - Breaking free from negative habits, behaviors, links, and patterns.
  - Gaining profound insights into your behavior paves the way for powerful change.

Bonus Resources:

Sign up for the valuable FREE Bonus Companion Course to help guide you meticulously through each of the 7 Hacksters, including video demonstrations of each technique throughout the workbook. Imagine unraveling your anxiety-ridden behavior and having the tools to rearrange them and then piece them back together so they work effectively for you with your therapist to guide you.

The course also contains downloadable worksheets, content, templates, and bonus video demonstrations of each technique revealed throughout each Hackster. To sign up for the course go to:

https://anxietyhacks.info/info-step1/

WARNING* *IMPORTANT* *WARNING

Suppose you've been triggered by reading something in your workbook and feel you want to slip back into your negative behaviors. Before you do anything else, I want you to immediately zip to Step 8 and immerse yourself in the Emotional Freedom Technique's (EFT) wisdom. This invaluable technique is your lifeline to navigate through emotional turbulence and reduce its grip on you.

WARNING* *CAUTION* *WARNING

ICONS

You will find four icons repeated throughout the workbook. So, when these pop up, I want you to pay extra attention.

When you see this icon, please think of a positive phrase you can repeat to yourself to fan your fire and propel your motivation forward. For example: "I am taking the steps to break free from anxiety forever."

When this icon appears, you will have a steaming hot tip to think about clearly.

When this icon pops up, it's time for you to reread and think about what you have learned.

For this icon, it's time to be super proud of yourself; you will have completed a valuable technique.

Breathing Exercises

At the beginning of each Hackster, you'll discover a powerful breathing technique waiting to be unleashed.

How Breathing Exercises Work:

Your Nervous System's Backdoor:

Imagine breathing exercises like a secret passageway to your nervous system, specifically the part that kicks into gear when you're stressed or anxious – it's called the sympathetic nervous system (SNS), which we will be learning more about in Hackster 2.

Controlling the Stress Patterns:

When your SNS becomes active, your heart rate, blood pressure, and breathing all speed up – classic anxiety symptoms. With these breathing techniques at the start of each Hackster, you can take the reins on your breathing, slowing it down and deepening it. This calms the stress response and flips the switch on other systems that make you feel calm and relaxed.

As you experiment with each breathing technique, you will learn to tweak your breathing, and you're basically telling anxiety to take a back seat. This change doesn't just affect your feelings. It works against the whole stress package – emotional, mental, hormonal, and even physical.

In a nutshell, if we had one, mastering your breath is like having a superpower against stress!

As we step into the pages of the Anxiety Hacks Workbook, let's shed light on anxiety – a complex dance of emotions, thoughts and body responses. It's more than just everyday worries; anxiety is a knotted experience we're here to explore together.

The Anxiety Hacks Workbook, packed with effective techniques, tips and tools, is your ticket to freedom from anxiety's grasp. It will become your guide, addressing the immediate effects of anxiety and delving into its origins. In Hackster 1, we dive into the very fabric of anxiety, unraveling its triggers and providing tools to navigate the intricate emotional landscape.
Beyond being a guide, this workbook is your pathway to self-discovery and empowerment. Are you ready to untangle the threads of anxiety, gaining a profound understanding of the inner workings of your mind?

Are you ready to free yourself from anxiety and reveal the calm, confident and empowered version of yourself? The journey doesn't start tomorrow; it kicks off right now. Ready to break free? The adventure awaits.

"Start where you are. Use what you have. Do what you can." - Arthur Ashe

HACKSTER 1

GROUNDING TOOLS WITH JEWELS

"Anxiety is a storm. You are the lighthouse. Shine bright, and guide yourself into calmness" – Kate Hudson-Hall

Congratulations on this Anxiety Hacks Workbook as your guide to overcoming anxiety and finding inner calm.

This Hackster is your toolkit introduction, equipping you with potent tools to dissect anxiety's roots, manage stress and build resilience. Uncover insights into common anxiety types, symptoms and causes. Get ready to boost your toolbox for a journey towards lasting calm and control. Let's begin the transformation.

What You'll Learn in Hackster 1:

In Hackster 1, you'll begin your journey of self-discovery and change. You will explore the key aspects of anxiety, gaining a complete understanding of what anxiety is, the various types of anxiety disorders and how it affects your life. We'll delve into the roots of your anxiety, helping to identify potential causes, triggers and symptoms connected with it.

Here's a sneak peek of what else lies ahead:

Understanding Anxiety: You'll learn what anxiety is, how it's a natural part of your everyday life and when it becomes a problem.

Common Types of Anxiety Disorders: Explore different anxiety disorders so you can recognize them in your life or the lives of those around you.

Symptoms of Anxiety: Discover the various ways anxiety can manifest physically and emotionally, helping you identify it more successfully.

What is an anxiety attack and what is a panic attack: Distinguish between anxiety and panic attacks, understanding their differences.

What Causes Anxiety: Explore potential triggers for anxiety, which may include past experiences, stress, abuse, trauma, and so much more.

Self-Reflection on anxiety: Complete a series of questions designed to help you identify your unique anxiety patterns.

Submodalities: Discover the role of submodalities in thinking and feeling, which you'll use to reprogram your unconscious mind.

By the end of Hackster 1, you'll have a foundation for a journey to self-improvement and anxiety reduction. You'll have essential tools and knowledge to help you tackle anxiety head-on and begin on the pathway to a calmer and more peaceful you. So, let's get started on this life-changing adventure together.

Serene Breaths Unleashed: Dive into tranquility with Hackster 1's signature technique!

Discover Serenity: ZenNose Breathing

ZenNose breathing is also known as Alternate Nostril Breathing. With this type of nasal breathing, you will gently alternate nostrils during slow and deliberate inhalation and exhalation. ZenNose breathing goes beyond helping unblock sinuses and enhancing breath-focused mindfulness.

Prepare for serenity:

Find a comfortable seated position. Exhale fully through both nostrils to prepare for the rhythmic practice.

Inhale through the Left Nostril:

Seal the right nostril with the right thumb and inhale deeply through the left nostril. Allow the breath to flow with intention.

Exhale through the Right Nostril:

At the peak of the inhale, release the right nostril and use the left forefinger to block the left nostril. Exhale through the right nostril.

Inhale through the Right Nostril:

Inhale through the right nostril, then switch back to blocking the right nostril. Continue the pattern, exhaling through the left nostril.

Repeat for mindful Harmony:

Continue this alternating pattern for as long as it feels beneficial. Follow these steps to unlock a pathway to serenity and focus.

Breathing exercises can improve sleep quality, promoting a sense of calmness and restfulness

What is this codswalloping anxiety malarky all about?

Understanding Anxiety

- Anxiety is a normal, natural feeling of worry, fear, or nervousness about upcoming events that we all experience.
- It is common to feel anxious in situations like exams, interviews, presentations or going on that first date.
- It only rears its ugly head occasionally and does not disrupt our daily life.

When Anxiety Becomes a Problem:

- Anxiety becomes a problem when high anxiety levels are present for a long time.
- It could be an anxiety disorder if your anxiety lasts longer than six months.

Common Types of Anxiety Disorders:

Generalized Anxiety Disorder (GAD) This is when you feel anxious about a wide range of issues rather than one specific problem.

Separation Anxiety Disorder: Fear of being separated from a caregiver most commonly happens in young children, but adults can experience this, too.

Panic Disorder: Unexplained and repeated panic attacks with emotional and physical symptoms.

Phobia: Irrational fears of specific situations, activities or objects.

OCD (Obsessive-Compulsive Disorder): Unwanted thoughts that lead to compulsive behaviors. It is often the result of a past traumatic event whereby the person relives the experience through nightmares or flashbacks, causing them to feel fearful, stressed, and unsafe even when they are safe.

Health or Illness Anxiety Disorder: This is excessively worrying you are or may become seriously ill but have no physical symptoms.

WHAT ARE THE SYMPTOMS OF ANXIETY?

Anxiety feels different for everyone, ranging from flapping butterflies in your stomach to your heart feeling like it is exploding out of your chest. You might feel there's a detachment between your powerful mind and body.

Other ways people experience anxiety include panic attacks, nightmares, and painful thoughts or memories that overwhelm them and are impossible to control. You may have a familiar feeling of fear and worry about a specific place or event.

Common symptoms of anxiety include:

Physical symptoms

- Digestive issues
- Increased heart rate
- Rapid breathing
- Trembling or muscle twitching
- Increase in heavy sweating
- Restlessness
- Headaches
- Poor immune system

Emotional symptoms

- Nervousness/tension
- Anticipating the worst
- Irritability
- Feelings and watching for signs of danger, panic, or dread
- Trouble concentrating
- Difficulty falling asleep
- Feel like your mind's gone blank

What is an anxiety attack?

Anxiety attacks gradually build up and are usually linked to anticipating a stressful situation, experience, or event. An attack occurs when anxiety increases to the point it gets in the way of your life and is part of the emotional and protective responses hardwired into the human body as you worry there may be some sort of threat ahead.

When anxiety is extreme or gets in the way of your life, there is cause for concern. Symptoms could last for days, weeks, or even months.

What is a panic attack?

Panic attacks come on suddenly, without an apparent cause, and include an overwhelming, intense fear accompanied by physical and mental symptoms. Your heartbeat booms, you find it difficult to breathe, and you may feel sick.

Unlike anxiety attacks, where your symptoms can last for a long time, panic attacks may last for ten minutes and begin to decrease. Still, it is not uncommon for several panic attacks to happen one after the other, making them feel like they last much longer than they do.

People often think anxiety attacks and panic attacks are the same things, but let me explain. They have very similar symptoms, but the main difference is panic attacks come on suddenly while anxiety attacks build gradually.

What is the difference between an anxiety attack and a panic attack?

WHAT CAUSES ANXIETY?

This is such a good question, which many of my clients ask me, but unfortunately, it differs from person to person. Some significant factors have been identified and may be familiar to people with anxiety. Let's take a looky look.

Triggers of anxiety are a huge contributing factor to anxiety and are so individual. We will talk more specifically about how to identify your triggers in Hackster 3, but here are some more common ones:

- Past experiences from childhood, teenage years, or as an adult.
- Experiencing significant stress, possibly due to work, personal or life-related factors.
- Physical or emotional abuse can have a lasting impact on your anxiety levels.
- Trauma such as neglect, death of a parent, being bullied, or being socially excluded can also be triggers.

For me, it was the summer I turned sixteen, left boarding school, and moved to live in downtown London on my own, knowing no one. I felt lonely and isolated. I started a new job. My mother sold the family house, relocated, and got remarried. Plus, I still had to lug around the burden of the big secret I had buried. At age 9, I was sexually abused. It was such a traumatic time for me, and my anxiety was paralyzing.

How to explore the root of *your* anxiety

Let's learn about you and your anxiety to gain a deeper understanding of your patterns.

Answering these questions will help you to reflect on your recent experiences of anxiety, gain insight into your anxiety patterns and recognize the core characteristics of your anxiety. Creating self-awareness and providing a foundation for further exploration and growth as you follow through the workbook.

Getting to the foundation of your anxiety begins by managing your anxiety symptoms so you can start thinking more clearly and self-reflecting.

Think about your recent experience of feeling anxious. To get a clear understanding of your patterns, please answer in as much detail as possible the following questions:

Do you feel like your anxiety is much more intense than others in everyday situations? If the answer is yes, write down three examples:

____

____

____

Does your anxiety stop you from engaging in certain events? If the answer is yes, list what they are.

____

____

____

Do you find that you focus on the worst-case scenario? If the answer is yes, list three examples.

____

____

____

Write down a recent situation where you felt a strong sense of anxiety. What do you believe triggered this feeling?

____

____

How intense was your anxiety on a scale of 1 to 10? (10 being the most intense.)

____

What were the physical sensations you experienced during that intense experience? (e.g., sweating, heart racing.)

____

____

What negative thoughts blew into your mind during this episode of anxiety?

____

____

Did you notice any changes in your breathing pattern? Was it irregular, fast or shallow?

____

____

How did your body posture change during this experience of anxiety? Were you fidgeting, tense, hunched over?

____

____

Were your thoughts solely focused on the anxiety, or were you able to focus on anything else during this anxious moment?

____

____

How did this episode of anxiety affect your overall mood and emotions? Did you feel more irritable, overwhelmed or sad?

Keeping in mind these experiences with anxiety, can you identify any patterns or triggers that contribute to such intense anxiety episodes in your life?

By answering these questions, you'll gain insights into the core characteristics of your severe anxiety episodes and develop a deeper understanding of how anxiety manifests in different situations.

Common Causes of Anxiety

To further understand your anxiety patterns, delving into the causes of your anxiety is crucial in your journey to lasting relief. It's like finding the key to unlock a door. It's essential for your journey to a calmer, happier you. When you know the causes, you can start addressing them head-on. This awareness empowers you to develop strategies to make choices to manage your anxiety more effectively. So, understanding the reasons behind your anxiety is your first step towards taking control of your life and breaking free from its tight grip.

In my journey, I discovered certain traumatic events from my past were the hidden sources of my anxiety. It was through this self-discovery that I started to understand and address my anxiety effectively.

In Hackster 3, we'll dig even deeper into the process of identifying your unique anxiety triggers and the strategies for managing them. Remember, the first step is awareness, and with every page you turn, you're gaining greater insight into your anxiety and the path to a calmer you.

What could be causing your anxiety?

- Worries about your loved ones,
- Enormous stress and exhaustion,
- Having to work long hours,
- Losing a job,
- Being abused or bullied,
- The death of your loved one,
- Unhealthy diet,
- Lots of change and uncertainty,
- Difficulties in your relationships,
- Fear of being separated from a loved one,
- Overload of pressure from work or studying,
- Financial issues,
- Physical health issues such as living with cancer, a heart problem or other physical health symptoms,
- Mental health issues such as depression, an eating disorder, or
- Medications, as sometimes this can be a side effect of taking the drug—it would be a good idea to check with your health care provider.

Anxiety doesn't just pop up out of nowhere. It's usually the result of a mix of different things happening in your life. To help you understand this, I've put together a table of the typical areas that can cause anxiety.

This table is your starting point for identifying and understanding the potential causes of your anxiety. As you go through it, consider how these factors might be at play in your life. By recognizing the triggers specific to your situation, you'll be better equipped to address them effectively.

Read through the list and see what patterns you can relate to:

Identifying the Causes of Your Anxiety

Causes of Anxiety	Common Symptoms	Impact	Prevention and Management
Worrying about your loved ones	Restlessness, Insomnia	Moderate	Regular communication with your loved ones, mindfulness practice
Overwhelmed with stress and exhaustion	Fatigue, Irritability	Severe	Start regular exercise stress reduction techniques
Unhealthy diet	Digestive issues, fatigue	Moderate	Create a balanced meal plan, and consult a nutritionist
Financial strain	Insomnia, constant worrying	Severe	Create a financial plan and budget
Difficulties in your relationships	Guilt, isolation	High	Make time for open communication, couples counseling
Being abused or bullied	Social anxiety, low self-worth	Severe	Establish boundaries, look for a therapist and work on self-esteem
A lot of change and uncertainty	Worry, indecision	Moderate	Stress reduction techniques, mindfulness
Overload of pressure from studying or work	Exhaustion, burnout	High	Time management, stress management techniques
Fear of being separated from a loved one	Constant worry, panic attacks, nightmares	Severe	Self-soothing techniques, find support groups
The death of a loved one	Overwhelming grief, sadness	Severe	Grief counseling, support groups

Now, you've gone through the list of common causes of anxiety and started to connect the dots. (Whoever dot is!) Now list your potential anxiety causes, common symptoms you have experienced, the impact it has had and what you can do to help.

Causes of Anxiety	Common Symptoms	Impact	Prevention and Management

Having completed this table of your common causes, symptoms, their impact and started to think about different ideas of how you can begin to break these patterns. Maybe you have identified potential triggers, recognized the symptoms they're linked to, and understood how they impact your life.

This self-awareness is your secret weapon

You can take charge by working on strategies to manage these patterns and reduce their hold. Remember, you're not alone on this journey; every small step forward counts. Your future self will thank you for making this effort.

"It does not matter how slowly you go as long as you do not stop" – **Confucius**

WHAT ARE SUBMODALITIES AND HOW TO USE THEM

Okay, buckle up and get ready to dive into the wacky world of submodalities! These little rascals are the building blocks of thinking, feeling and reacting to things. Think of them as the superheroes of your mind, ready to swoop in and save the day by helping you reprogram your unconscious mind and transform the way you feel and think.

Now it's time to put on your detective hat, become a master of your thoughts, and listen to what you are saying to yourself.

You see, when it comes to thinking, we've got options. It's like a buffet of mental activities. We can think in pictures, words, feelings, and even tastes and smells get in on the action. It's a wild party up in our brains.

Let's have a little thought experiment. Picture this: I ask you, "What color is your phone cover?" Now, take a moment and let the mental chaos unfold. You might see an image of your phone, think about its color or even experience a feeling about it. It's like a metal game show where the prize is… well, the answer to the question.

But hang on, there's more! Get ready to enter and use the zany world of submodalities. These bad boys come in five flavors, each corresponding to one of our senses. We've got:

- visual submodalities for pictures
- auditory submodalities for sounds
- kinesthetic submodalities for feelings and
- gustatory and olfactory submodalities for tastes and smells.

So grab your mental popcorn and prepare for a mind-bending journey through the world of submodalities. It's time to unleash your inner Sherlock Holmes and uncover the secrets of your mind.

Submodalities Checklist for Anxiety Relief

Here, we have a list of the submodalities with a check box to complete to help you through many of the techniques throughout this workbook. To help you gain the most out of the techniques, make them as powerful as possible to reduce your anxiety.

Hop back to this table as you work through the different techniques when we use submodalities, for example, the "Calm New You Technique."

SUBMODALITIES TABLE

SUBMODALITIES GROUP	SUBMODALITIES TO CHANGE	TECHNIQUE	✓ USED
Visual Submodalities (Pictures) These are the pictures you have in your mind, which could be:	• In color or black and white • Disassociated: Are you in the picture looking through your own eyes (associated) or • Looking at the image as if it were a picture (disassociated)? • Close up or far away • Size of the picture A movie or still picture		
Auditory submodalities (Things you hear) These are what you hear; they may include:	• Words or sounds • Constant or intermittent • Loud or quiet • High or low pitch, Duration • Direction of the voice		
Kinesthetic submodalities (Feelings and sensations) These are your feelings and sensations; they may include:	• Location—where it is in the body • Shape or size • Intensity Temperature—hot or cold • Still or moving Breathing rate		
Gustatory and olfactory submodalities This is a taste and smell that may include:	• Sour • Sweet • Aroma – strength • Bitter • Fragrance		

Client Example: Learn How my client used submodalities to reduce her anxiety:

Meet Joanie, who was struggling with overwhelming anxiety triggered by going to social situations. Joanie often found herself paralyzed with fear and anxiety in group gatherings. As we learned about submodalites, she began to learn valuable insights that transformed her anxiety.

Identifying her triggers:

Joanie diligently used the submodalities table to understand the visual, auditory, kinesthetic, gustatory and olfactory aspects related to anxiety triggers, which in this case was a social event. She would vividly picture crowded rooms and judgemental voices, felt a tightness in her chest and associated a bitter taste with her anxiety.

Understanding her Visual Submodalities: (What she could see)

Color and Association: Joanie noticed the mental image of social events was in vivid colors, which intensified her anxiety. She was 'associated into the picture,' which means she was looking through her own eyes in the picture, not just looking at it.

Distance: The image was sometimes up close, making her feel overwhelmed.

Understanding her Auditory Submodalities: (What she could hear)

Volume and Pitch: The sound was loud and high-pitched, causing a sense of chaos.

Constant Nature: The sounds seemed constant without any breaks.

Understanding Kinestetic Submodalieits: (What she felt)

Location and intensity: The feeling in her chest was intense, in the center, intensifying her emotional distress.

Temperature: She was very hot and sweaty.

Understanding Gustatory and Olfactory: (What she could taste and smell)

Bitter Taste: Joanie had a bitter taste in her mouth, adding a negative layer to her anxiety.

Following is how Joanie used Submodalities to Reduce her Anxiety:

Changing Visual Submodalities: We worked on changing the color to a calming green, moving the image further away, making it a still picture rather than a moving scent, and she stepped out of the picture. This immediately reduced the intensity of her anxiety.

Changing Auditory Submodalities: Joanie practiced lowering the volume and pitch of the sound in her mind, initiating moments of silence to create a sense of calm.

Changing Kinestectic Submodalities: By moving the feeling from the center of her chest to a more peripheral location and changing the temperature to neutral, Joanie felt a significant reduction in the physical feelings of her anxiety.

Changing Custatory and Olfactory Submodalities: She worked on replacing the bitter taste with something more pleasant, slightly sweet taste. Associating a pleasant fragrance with the imagined scenario.

Joanie's Results: Joanie consistently employed these submodality techniques over several sessions. As a result, she reported a remarkable decrease in her anxiety levels during social events. The past overwhelming and paralyzing scenes in her mind transformed into manageable, even positive mental images. Joanie rewired her unconscious mind through the power of submodalities, paving the way for a more confident and relaxed approach to social situations.

> **"The only limit to our realization of tomorrow will be our doubts of today"** - **Franklin D. Roosevelt**

ANXIETY THERMOMETER SCALE

So, to begin to break down your negative pattern, let me introduce the anxiety thermometer scale. This is a scale you can use to gauge where you are with your anxiety bundle of stress.

It is a scale from 0 to 10.

- **0 is when the anxiety has vanished completely.**
- **10 is when it is most intense or a panic attack.**

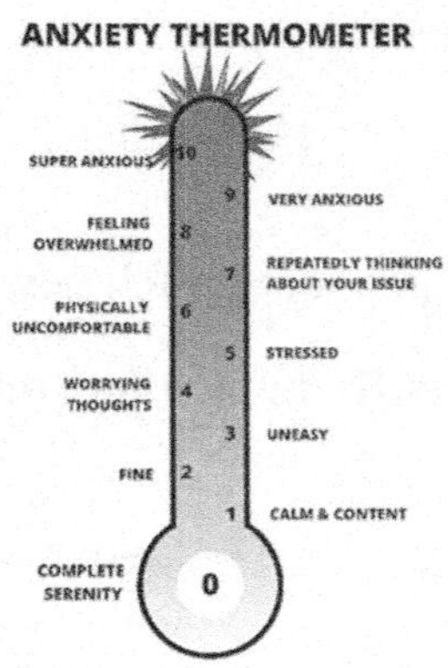

ANXIETY DIARY WITH YOUR NEW THERMOMETER SCALE

You have answered the questions about the causes of your anxiety. Now, create your anxiety diary so you can use to track fluctuations in your anxiety over time.

Why keep an anxiety diary?

Keeping a detailed anxiety diary will help you:

- Begin to understand your triggers, negative thought patterns and feeling fluctuations related to life events and medication changes.
- By consistently writing down your anxious experiences, you can begin to understand in greater depth the causes and patterns of your anxiety, which will help you understand yourself and your patterns better.

- Regularly completing your diary will provide concrete/clear records of your progress. Reviewing previous entries, you can become more aware of your positive changes, how your anxiety levels have changed, and identify what works and doesn't work so well and your progress. All of which can boost your motivation and confidence in your ability to deal with your anxiety patterns.
- Begin to release much of the pent-up emotions connected to your anxiety. Writing about your anxious thoughts and feelings can provide a safe space to express and process your feelings and emotions. Plus, it can serve as a positive release.

Remember, awareness is the first step that empowers you to develop targeted coping strategies and make informed choices in managing your anxiety.

How to get started with your diary

Create a system that works for you.

In this example of an anxiety diary, you could download and print out or copy into:

- A diary or journal,
- The ol' computer
- Your phone, or find an app to chart your anxiety
- Even plain paper, or
- Toilet paper!

I really don't mind! So, think about which would be the most convenient for you and get creative.

What you could do differently next time you have anxiety: What could you change next time your trigger fires up your anxiety?

Scale: Rate where you are on your anxiety thermometer scale from 0 to 10.

Complete the anxiety diary as and when you feel your anxiety rising. This is a crucial tool in your arsenal for managing anxiety. It will empower you to take control of your thoughts and feelings, recognize your triggers and ultimately work towards a calmer, happier you.

ANXIETY DIARY

DATE AND TIME	YOUR TRIGGERS (WHAT INCREASES THE ANXIETY)	SYMPTOMS (EMOTIONAL & PHYSICAL IN THE BODY?)	NEGATIVE THOUGHTS/ IMAGES	OUTCOME (WHAT HAPPENED AS A CONSEQUENCE?)	WHAT YOU COULD DO DIFFERENTLY NEXT TIME YOU HAVE ANXIETY	RATE ON A SCALE FROM 0 TO 10
Example:	Work colleague's negative behavior toward me. TRIGGER: Seeing two colleagues chatting	FEELING: anxious/fearful/nervous PHYSICAL: tense/sweating/having a sense of impending embarrassment	THOUGHT: "I can't go to the meeting and speak. My colleagues will make fun of me." IMAGE: of meeting sitting around a table and colleagues smirking at me.	I did it and felt fine. No one laughed at me	Be aware of what I am thinking and bat those negative thoughts into oblivion	**10**
Monday						
Tuesday						
Wednesday						
Thursday						
Friday						
Saturday						
Sunday						

By keeping up to date with your anxiety diary, you will become the anxiety equivalent of a weather forecaster: You'll predict your anxiety storms better than the weather forecast predicts rain. "I can see a 75% chance of anxiety around 3 pm. Better bring an umbrella of coping strategies."

TECHNIQUE: THE "CALM NEW YOU TECHNIQUE"

Are you ready to learn how to begin to reprogram your mind to feel calmer? Yessss, here we go . . .

By reinforcing positive self-images with powerful, positive feelings, you start to teach your brain you want to change and bring more things that are more enjoyable and make you feel better. If you don't believe me, try this out for yourself!

Listen up because your ears never stop growing! It is time to start to get your motivation going and begin reprograming your mind now to think differently and positively and draw you away from your anxiety:

Read through all the steps to know where you're going with this. I don't want you to get lost!

Step	Action
1.	First, imagine how you would like to be in the future, free from anxiety. What would you be doing, thinking, feeling, saying to yourself? Happy, healthy, excited, free.
2.	Look at all the details of how you would look: standing upright, feeling confident, calm, smiling, positive, and happy.
3.	Now, make this image or movie as powerful as possible, using your new skill of changing the submodalities of your image. Go through your list of submodalities and make this picture as empowering as possible, changing it as follows: • Make the colors brighter and bolder. • Make the image life-size or bigger, if possible. • What would you be saying to yourself? "I'm finally calm and living the life I've always dreamed of." • How would you be feeling? Motivated, relaxed, empowered, and excited for your new future? • Change the movie if needed so it's the most empowering movie you've ever watched.
4.	Now, step into this incredible new you, so you're actually in the picture, looking through your own eyes, feeling what you'll be feeling after not having had anxiety for months or even years. What are you saying to yourself? Something like, "I'm relaxed and free and so proud of myself." Now, intensify the feelings, making them as big and powerful as possible.
5.	How would you be feeling? Motivated, relaxed, empowered, and excited for your new future?

To get copies of the tables and watch extra videos where I show each technique, join the Bonus Companion Course: https://anxietyhacks.info/info-step1/

You did it! I want you to step into "The Calm New You" every morning and evening and periodically throughout each day. Repetition is the key to your achievement. You're reprogramming your unconscious mind, reminding it of the positive direction you want to go in, which will help you focus on it.

If you don't believe me, try it out. What have you got to lose? It works! You'll start to see, hear, and feel a new, calm, empowered you. It will help you incredibly to begin to change.

So you can check how often you are stepping into your image and when. Complete this table daily to keep reminding yourself to step into your image and reap the rewards of your unconscious mind assisting you in changing your anxious behaviors.

The Calm New You Tracker

Day of the Week	**When to Step into Image**	**How often?**
Example:	Whenever I walk into the kitchen	Five times
Monday		
Tuesday		
Wednesday		
Thursday		
Friday		
Saturday		
Sunday		
Monday		
Tuesday		
Wednesday		
Thursday		
Friday		
Saturday		
Sunday		
Monday		
Tuesday		
Wednesday		
Thursday		
Friday		
Saturday		
Sunday		
Monday		
Tuesday		
Wednesday		
Thursday		
Friday		
Saturday		
Sunday		

"Your present circumstances don't determine where you can go; they merely determine where you start" - Nido Qubein

EXTRA TOOLS FOR YOUR TOOLBOX TO A CALMER YOU

In this Hackster, you've learned a vast amount of information on anxiety to help you guide you on your pathway to reduce anxiety as you weave your way through this workbook.

The key takeaways you have learned are:

Understanding Anxiety

- What anxiety is and how it is a normal, natural feeling of worry, fear or nervousness about up-and-coming events that we all experience.
- The everyday situations where anxiety is felt, the difference between occasional vs chronic anxiety and common types of anxiety disorders.

What causes anxiety and the Symptoms of Anxiety

- How anxiety can manifest differently with descriptions of various ways anxiety is experienced physically and mentally.
- A variety of factors contribute to anxiety, for example, stress, personal experiences, abuse and trauma.

Self-Reflection on Anxiety

- Completing the series of questions, you can begin to understand personal patterns of anxiety and how it impacts your daily life, physical sensations, thoughts, feelings and behaviors.
- Learned how to identify your anxiety triggers, listing common triggers that impact your life and prevention and management strategies for each. Also, create a table to list your potential anxiety causes, symptoms and management strategies.

Anxiety Thermometer Scale and Diary

- An introduction to the anxiety Thermometer Scale from 0 to 10 to gauge your anxiety.
- The importance of keeping a diary and suggestions on how to maintain your diary with an example table format for entries.

What Submodalities Are and How to Use Them

- Understanding what submodalities are for sensory perception (visual, auditory, kinesthetic, gustatory and olfactory.)
- A table to track changes in submodalities to help you change your patterns and behaviors.

The Calm New You Technique

- You were introduced to the "Calm New You Technique," with a step-by-step guide to reprogram your mind and become calm.
- A table to track when and how often you step into the fantastic "Calm New You" image.

"It's not the load that breaks you down, it's the way you carry it" - Lou Holtz

Review and Reflection:

Answer these questions to help you understand what you have learned in this Hackster and how you can use it to create a calmer you:

Understanding Anxiety

- Describe what anxiety is and give three examples of everyday situations when you experience anxiety.

____

____

____

- Can you remember a time when anxiety didn't disrupt your daily life and only popped up occasionally?

____

____

What causes anxiety and the Symptoms of Anxiety

- What do you think might be some common causes of your anxiety? How do you handle these triggers?

____

____

- If you have experienced trauma or difficult past events, how do you believe they influence your anxiety today?

Self-Reflection on Anxiety

- What have you learned about your specific anxiety patterns?

- What and how are you going to begin to break your anxiety behaviors?

Anxiety Thermometer Scale and Diary

- How are you going to use the Anxiety Thermometer Scale to understand and manage your anxiety each day?

- What specific actions will you take when you find your anxiety spiraling?

What Submodalities Are and How to Use Them

- What have you learned about submodalities?

- How will you use the submodalities table to make the techniques more powerful for managing your anxiety?

The Calm New You Technique

- List the specific times of the day or situations when you will be stepping into the "Calm New You" image.

- How will you set up reminders to keep you on track?

Hackster 1: And Finally:

As we wrap up Hackster 1 understanding of anxiety, we've just scratched the surface of the intricate world of anxiety. You've now begun to equip yourself with the tools to recognize common anxiety disorders, understand the symptoms and even delve into the root of your personal anxiety through thoughtful questions. Skip along to Hackster 2, and let's unravel the mysteries of stress – good, bad and ugly. Learn how stress and anxiety intertwine, and learn practical tools to address your stressors.

"Do not anticipate trouble or worry about what may never happen. Keep in the sunlight" - **Benjamin Franklin**

HACKSTER 2

THE UNEXPECTED PROBLEM WITH ANXIETY = UNDERSTANDING STRESS

"Strength does not come from the body. It comes from the will" - Unknown

What You'll Learn in Hackster 2:

Stress is connected with your anxiety.

In this second hackster of your anxiety-busting toolbox, we're delving into the complex relationship between your anxiety and stress. But here's the twist: anxiety doesn't stand alone. It's a partner in crime with stress. It would help if you dismantled this formidable duo to equip you with the tools and understanding.

Here's a sneak peek of what else lies ahead:

1. **What is stress?**

- We'll break down the concept of stress, from the good to the bad to the downright ugly.
- You'll learn how stress can be both your ally and your enemy.

2. **The Stressometer Table**

- To start things off, here's a handy tool to help you gauge your stress levels. It's like a thermometer for your mind, and you will learn how to use it effectively.

3. **The Nervous System**
   - It's time to unlock the mysteries of your nervous system. So get ready for an adventure into the inner workings of your body and mind.

4. **What is Stressing You Out?**
   - You will be provided with a stress trigger checklist and ideas to tackle these triggers head-on.

5. **The Breathe Not Seethe Technique**
   - Discover a powerful breathing technique that can help you keep stress at bay. We'll provide you with a table to track your progress.

6. **The For Your Eyes Only Technique**
   - For those moments when anxiety starts to creep in, you'll learn a discrete technique to manage your thoughts. Track your successes in our handy table.

   But wait, there's more!

   In " The Unexpected Problem with Anxiety!, you'll find answers to questions like:

- *What exactly is stress?*
- *How does it connect to anxiety, and why does that connection matter?*
- *How can you take control of your stress and, in turn, your anxiety?*

So prepare to unravel the intricate web of stress and anxiety as we equip you with strategies and insights to emerge stronger and calmer on the other side.

Serene Breaths Unleashed: Dive into tranquility with Hackster 2's signature technique!

Embark on Tranquillity: The "BreathEase Technique"

The BreathEase Technique integrates deep breathing and visualization, providing a powerful tool to alleviate stressors and anxiety. The good news is the entire exercise only takes six seconds, so it is perfect for anyone on the go.

Prepare for serenity:

Wherever you are, whether on a train, plane or automobile, begin by relaxing all face and shoulder muscles. Then, imagine you have holes in the soles of your feet.

Inhale with Visualization:

Take a deep breath while visualizing the breath as warm air gracefully entering your body through the imagined holes in the soles of your feet.

Flow of Warmth:

Picture the warm air flowing upward, traveling through your leg's, abdominal area and finally filling your lungs. Feel the soothing warmth as it touches each muscle along its pathway.

Muscle Relaxation:

As the warm air passes each muscle, consciously relax it, allowing the calming sensation to pass through.

Exhale Slowly with Imagery:

Exhale gradually, envisioning the air flowing from your lungs back into the abdominal area, then down through the legs before leaving your body through the holes in the soles of your feet.

Repeat for Calmness:

Continue with this rhythmic practice until a sense of calmness floods over you. Repeat The "BreathEase Technique" to continue deepening your relaxation.

Immerse yourself in the art of tranquillity with The "BreathEase Technique" – a harmonious blend of intentional breath and visualization.

Deep breathing helps to control emotions by soothing the amygdala, which is like the brain's emotion hub.

WHAT EXACTLY IS STRESS?

Stress is like a pressure cooker: It builds up slowly and, if not released, can lead to an explosive situation. We all deal with it, and it comes in many forms. Although a small amount of stress can be very beneficial, it is like a personal trainer pushing you to achieve your best in the gym.

Stress happens when it feels like life throws too much your way, and you are unsure you can handle it. It's the feeling of being pulled in all directions, mentally and emotionally.

THE UPSIDE – GOOD STRESS

Good stress is also known as Eustress. Think of this as the hero version of stress propelling you to perform at your best. It's your body's way of preparing you for something exciting.

Good stress can help you:

- Jump into a challenging project.
- Stay super focused when your social media is calling.
- Venture out on a first date.

In an emergency, good stress can give you the strength to deal with difficult situations. It's like the sweep of adrenaline rush that fades away once the excitement decreases.

THE DOWNSIDE – BAD STRESS:

Bad stress is when our stress levels turn dark, leaving us feeling tense, nervous and incapable of handling whatever may be tossed our way. When the stressful situation ends, you don't feel as if you can bounce back to your usual sprightly self.

Bad stress can lead to:

Reaching out for alcohol, cigarettes or comfort food,

Experiencing anxiety, feeling irritable, tired or persistent headaches.

Our bodies aren't wired to endure non-stop bad stress. It can seriously affect your health, mood and relationships.

THE UGLY TRUTH – UGLY STRESS

This is when stress goes full speed ahead and is like being on a never-ending anxiety rollercoaster.

Ugly stress can lead to severe problems like:

- High blood pressure,
- Packing on extra pounds,
- feeling exhausted or having trouble sleeping,
- Debilitating headaches, muscle tension or shaking,
- Even affects your love life.

Ugly stress doesn't just dampen your spirits; it severely threatens your overall health. It weakens your immune system and can lead to serious chronic illness.

THE TAKEAWAY

So now you know a small amount of stress each day can give you a little boost. But when it hangs around for too long, it's time to start being more aware of your stress patterns and finding the right tools to reduce your stress levels.

HOW IS STRESS CONNECTED TO YOUR ANXIETY?

Let's break down the link between stress and anxiety. Unfortunately, many of us have experienced the trauma of severe stress and anxiety at some point. Let's be honest. Our lives are brimming with stress. It's like the unwelcome guest who loves to spring up when you least expect it.

Stress vs. Anxiety

- Stress is your body's way of reacting to life's challenges, and it is normal and can sometimes motivate you.
- Anxiety is like stress's evil twin hanging around even after a stressful event has passed. It's like stress on steroids.

Why It Matters

- Stress is like the ignition switch for anxiety. It often fires anxiety into gear.
- Having a clear understanding of your stress and how it connects to your anxiety is like having a secret weapon to manage both.

Managing Stress

- You can't escape stress altogether – it's part of life's package.
- But you can learn how to handle stress, which is the key. It's like conquering your favorite game: you are more likely to win once you know the rules.

The main differences between stressful situations where both stress and anxiety overlap and then the anxiety itself. The key is understanding these differences to manage and address these emotional states.

	Stress	Both stress and anxiety	Anxiety	How can you relate?
Response origin	• Normally, a response to an **external cause,** such as an argument with a friend or taking an exam • Disappears once the situation is resolved • Could be negative or positive. Such as: Cause tension or headaches or motivate you to present the perfect speech	Both stress and anxiety can affect your body and mind. Symptoms you may experience: Tension • Headaches • Blood pressure rising • Over worrying • Lack of sleep	• Normally, it is internal. It's your reaction to stress • Generally, it creates feelings of dread or worry that won't go away and affects how you live your life • It is always there even after the event when there is no threat	

"The only person you are destined to become is the person you decide to be" - Ralph Waldo Emerson

UNLOCKING THE MYSTERIES OF YOUR NERVOUS SYSTEM

Let's unravel the mysteries of the fascinating world of your nervous system.

Born Anxiety – Free

Your anxiety isn't hardwired into you. It's a pattern developed over time. It's like vines multiplying in your garden.

Your brain misreads everyday situations as dangerous when there isn't any triggering anxiety.

The Anxiety Loop

- It's like a broken record. Imagine your brain as a vintage vinyl record. The big scratch on it causes it to replay the same anxious thought, never progressing to the next track.
- This unconsciously creates a loop of anxiety-provoking thoughts and feelings without you realizing it.

Understanding your Two Nervous Systems

You have two separate systems within your nervous system: the sympathetic and parasympathetic nervous systems. They both play a crucial role in how you react to stress and anxiety. Let's look further at the two.

The Sympathetic Nervous System and Anxiety

- When you're stressed due to, say, work pressure, financial worries or family issues, your body reacts with anxiety.
- The sympathetic nervous system is like the gas pedal on a car, pushing your body into a fight or flight response to keep you safe.
- Then, stress hormones like cortisol are released, causing sweating, a racing heart, or muscle tension.
- This natural response is designed for life-threatening experiences but happens even for non-life-threatening stressful events, leading to anxiety.

Fight or flight Feeling

- For example, this fight-or-flight feeling would be if you were in your garden tinkering with your prize-winning weeds (or even roses!) and suddenly, a lion jumped over the fence. Your survival mechanism swoops in to keep you safe, and you run for the hills - if you have a large enough garden.
- Unfortunately, it fires up everyday stressors, making you anxious.
- Then, once your brain realizes the danger has passed or there is no danger, it tries to calm you down through the parasympathetic nervous system.

The Parasympathetic Nervous System and Calmness

- The parasympathetic nervous system is like the breaks in a car and slows down the stress response.
- It releases 'feel-good' hormones like serotonin to calm your mind and body.
- Realizing you are no longer in danger is when the parasympathetic nervous system hops and makes this happen.

Learning to understand these two systems can then help you take control of your anxiety and how you react to stress. This is similar to learning to lift that heavy foot off the gas pedal and create a calmer, weightless ride.

How to use your parasympathetic nervous system to control your stress and anxiety to feel calmer.

Unlocking Your Calm with the Parasympathetic Nervous System:

- When the parasympathetic nervous system ignites, it causes your mind and body to feel calm and at ease.
- Creating new habits and patterns is the key to controlling stress and anxiety, creating a calmer, more serene you.

What happens when the parasympathetic system activates

The parasympathetic system is like having a magic wand causing:

- Muscles to relax and release tension.
- Your breathing to slow down to its calmer natural rhythm.
- Heart rate drops, calming the racing feeling.
- Blood pressure to lower.

The outcome? A more peaceful state of mind and body - something we all crave.

Welcoming Calmness: How to fire up your parasympathetic nervous system:

- There are many techniques to stimulate your parasympathetic nervous system, many of which we will be delving into in this workbook, for example, the "Breathe Not Seeth Technique," "Mindfulness," reading, the "C.A.L.M. Your Alarm Technique."
- Consciously strengthening and activating your parasympathetic nervous system will immediately reduce your feelings of anxiety and stress, lower your blood pressure, and boost your immune system. Other ways to ignite your parasympathetic nervous system are:
- Mild exercise
- Mindfulness/ meditation
- Yoga
- Praying
- Take a hot bath
- Put on relaxing music
- Cuddle a pet or a human
- Sewing
- Drawing/doodling
- Reading
- Do absolutely nothing

So, now you have a clearer understanding of your nervous system, let's learn more about you, your stress, and beastly anxiety.

What is stressing you out right now? It could be:

- Family issues, difficulty in a relationship, or divorce,
- Moving to a new home,
- The death of a loved one,
- Unpaid bills,
- Chronic illness or injury,
- A traumatic event: theft, rape, violence toward you or a loved one, or
- Working long hours, too much responsibility, or losing your job.

It's time for you to take control of your life, as stress only becomes an issue when we don't manage it correctly. If not addressed, it will increase, as will your anxiety.

To address your stress patterns, here is a table of ideas to help you with your stress triggers. How many do you identify with?

Stress Trigger	**Ideas to Address the Trigger**	✓
Work-related stress	Create solid boundaries between personal life and work	
	Communicate freely with managers about workload	
	Manage time effectively, prioritizing tasks	
	Learn relaxation techniques to use at work	
Financial stress	Develop a budget and glue yourself to it	
	Create additional income sources	
	Take financial advice or therapy if needed	
Health-related stress	Look at your sleep routines and maintain a balanced diet	
	Create a positive exercise routine that works for you	
	Reach out to healthcare professionals for help and guidance	
Relationship issues	Explore couples or family therapy if necessary	
	Create healthy boundaries in relationships and remove the weeds	
	Learn how to practice active listening	
Environmental stressors	Reduce exposure to social media and negative news	
	Declutter your home to create a calmer environment	
	Take yourself out into nature to destress and reconnect	
General life pressures	Practice stress-reducing techniques	
	Seek therapy for coping strategies	

"Success is not final, failure is not fatal: It is the courage to continue that counts" - Winston Churchill

HOW TO MANAGE YOUR STRESS WITH THE STRESS-O-METER

How stressed are you right now?

Do you feel like you are thrashing around in the water, and no one can hear your cries, and you are sinking?

Stress is a heavy weight to lumber around on your shoulders, but you can begin to lift each layer off.

You have your anxiety scale, so let's learn to work with your stress levels with the stress-o-meter.

I would like you to rate where you are on the stress-o-meter scale each day. Write this in the table and start using your new breathing technique, the "Breathe, Not Seethe Technique," explained further in this Hackster. Create a new habit to calm you when you're feeling stressed.

STRESS-O-METER SCALE

This stress-o-meter scale is a scale from 0 to 10. 0 being when you are totally relaxed and calm.

10 being when you are absolutely stressed out or super scared.

THE STRESS-O-METER TABLE

List daily stressful events and rate where you are on the scale from 0 to 10. Create a guide similar to this table.

How stressed, anxious, scared, or tense do you feel?

The Stress-O-Meter Table:

THE STRESSFUL EVENT	MONDAY SCALE 0 - 10	TUESDAY SCALE 0 - 10	WEDNESDAY SCALE 0 - 10	THURSDAY SCALE 0 - 10	FRIDAY SCALE 0 - 10	SATURDAY SCALE 0 - 10	SUNDAY SCALE 0 - 10

TECHNIQUE: THE "BREATHE, NOT SEETHE TECHNIQUE"

You now understand the difference between your sympathetic and parasympathetic nervous systems. This is a super simple technique to use whenever your anxiety builds up.

It's time to learn to respond rather than react. You will feel more relaxed by following these steps and working with your parasympathetic nervous system.

The Breathe Not Seethe Technique Steps

Here we go; hold onto your hats (if you have one on!).

Step	Description	Steps
1.	Rate on the Stress-O-Meter Scale	Rate your current stress level from 0-10
2.	Take one deep breath	Inhale through your nose for a count of four all the way down to the base of your stomach
3.	Hold your breath	For a count of eight
4.	Exhale	Breathe out through your mouth for a count of eight. Purse your lips and blow out like blowing a candle or bubble
5.	Repeat	Repeat this two more times
6.	Reassess your stress level	Hop back to your stress-o-meter scale and check where you are
7.	Repeat	If you are not down to a 0, continue with your magical breathing steps

To watch extra videos where I show each technique, join the Bonus Companion Course at: https://anxietyhacks.info/info-

Practice the "Breathe, Not Seethe Technique" often throughout the day, especially when stressed, anxious, fearful, worried, or nervous. Work with your stress-o-meter and rate on the scale. If you rate 10, repeat this ten times.

Keep a log of how often you're practicing this to create a new positive habit, and then keep rating throughout the week. It's an excellent, super-fast way to clear your fuzzy mind and calm yourself immediately…AND BREATHE.

When you inhale deeply, it's like your brain receives a calm-down memo. Your brain then directs the message to your body. It's the ultimate relaxation hotline!

"Inhale, exhale, watch your worries set sail"

The Breathe, Not Seethe Technique Tracker:

Date/Time	**Location**	**Triggers**	**Physical Sensations**	**Thoughts and Feelings**	**Scale Before the Breathe Not Seethe Technique (0-10)**	**Scale After The Breathe Not Seethe Technique (0-10)**	**How I felt after**
Example	**Office**	**Disagreement with coworker**	**Tense, heart beating fast**	**'I am so frustrated I can't take it anymore'**	**10**	**4**	**Calmer, thinking more rationally**

TECHNIQUE: THE "FOR YOUR EYES ONLY TECHNIQUE"

For this technique, all you need is your eyes!

Another way to reduce your stressful and anxious thoughts is with the powerful "For Your Eyes Only Technique."

It is an excellent thought-stopping technique to help you manage anxiety caused by what is happening in your life or past events. Once you have learned the steps, you can use them for any stress that creates your anxiety and thoughts or specific fears.

It is so simple, and the advantage of this technique is no one will know what you are doing! So, if you are at an event, party, work, or anywhere else and feel super anxious, dip in and use this powerful technique from your toolbox.

Here are the steps to the simple tool to calm your anxiety.

For Your Eyes Only Technique Steps

Step	Instructions
1.	Identify your stressful, anxious thoughts or feelings. Tune in and become aware of the recurring thoughts, feelings, images, or memories intensifying your anxiety.
2.	Where are you on the Stress-o-meter scale? As you tune in to your stressful, anxious thoughts, feelings, or images, rate where you are on the Stress-o-meter scale.
3.	Here we go. . . For Your Eyes Only. . . Once you have rated where you are on your Stress-o-meter, keeping your head still, quickly move your eyes back and forth between two predetermined points twenty to twenty-five times while focusing on your anxiety. (For example: Between two sides of a desk, table, window, corners of a room, whatever works for you at that moment.)
4.	Then tell yourself to "Let Go." Relax your shoulders. Allow all the anxiety to drain from the top of your head down and out of your feet.
5.	Hop back to your Stress-o-meter scale and rate your stress and anxiety level between 0 – 10. This technique often blocks or rapidly reduces your ability to focus on a thought, feeling or image. Depending on where you are on the scale, the key is reducing the problematic thought, feeling or image to a 0.
6.	Repeat, Repeat, RRRRepeat Repeat steps 1–4 until it is down to a 0.

If you are in public and feel uncomfortable doing this with your eyes open, moving your eyes from side to side with your eyes closed is also super effective. Anyone might think you are taking a moment to yourself or thinking deeply.

Whenever you are aware of the anxiety beginning to build up, hop in and repeat this powerful technique. Keep repeating this every five minutes if you feel you need to.

Each time you hop in and repeat this technique, it becomes even more effective, and your overall anxiety will reduce powerfully.

To watch extra videos where I show each technique, join the Bonus Companion Course at: https://anxietyhacks.info/info-step1/

Client Example: Using the "Four Your Eyes Only Technique" to reduce anxiety

Meet John, a client of mine who was dealing with persistent anxiety related to a traumatic event from his past. He often found himself overwhelmed by intrusive thoughts and feelings associated with trauma. The "For Your Eyes Only Technique" became a discreet yet powerful tool in his anxiety management toolbox.

We identified the stressful thoughts: John and I worked to identify the recurring thoughts and feelings linked to the past traumatic event. These thoughts were vivid and intrusive and significantly contributed to his anxiety.

Stress-o-meter Rating:

John then rated his current anxiety level on the Stress-o-meer scale as a distressing 8 out of 10. His intrusive thoughts often led to panic attacks, and he felt helpless.

Now for the "For Your Eyes Only Technique":

The technique: John tuned into the traumatic thoughts and feelings and quickly moved his eyes back and forth between two fixed window points.

Letting Go:

Following the eye movement, he told himself to "Let Go." He consciously relaxed his shoulders and allowed the tension connected with his traumatic thoughts to drain away.

Post Technique Rating: John returned to the Stress-O-Meter scale after applying the technique. His anxiety level had dropped down to a manageable 4 out of 10.

Repetition and Reinforcement:

John repeated the process several times, each time experiencing a decrease in the intensity of the traumatic thoughts. I then encouraged John to use the technique whenever he felt his anxiety rising.

Adapting in Public:

As John became more comfortable with the technique, he adapted it for use in public spaces. He found closing his eyes and discreetly moving them from side to side helped to calm himself, allowing him to manage his anxiety without drawing attention to himself.

Long Term Benefits:

John consistently used the "For Your Eyes Only" technique for several weeks. His intrusive thoughts at times felt totally overwhelming but gradually lost their power. The overall anxiety connected with the past traumatic event significantly reduced, allowing John to engage more calmly in his daily life.

Conclusion:

The "For Your Eyes Only Technique" played a pivotal role in Johns's journey to overcoming his anxiety regarding his past traumatic experience. By including this technique in his daily routine and adapting it to different settings, he developed a valuable skill for addressing anxiety in different aspects of his life. Johns's story demonstrates the transformative power of a simple yet super-effective technique in reclaiming control over intrusive thoughts.

"Stay on track, and stress won't hold you back."

For Your Eyes Only Technique Log

This table is your personal guide to track the effectiveness of the "Four Your Eyes Only Technique." Record the date and time, note anxious thoughts and feelings, rate your stress level before and after (on a scale of 0-10) predetermined points for eye movement, log the number of eye movements, and jot down any additional notes. Use this log to tailor the technique to your unique journey.

For Your Eyes Only Technique Log Table:

Date/Time	Anxious Thoughts and Feelings	Stress Level Before (0-10)	Predetermined Points for Eye Movement	Number of Eye Movements	Stress Level After (0-10)	Notes
Example	Feeling anxious in a crowd	7	Corners of the room	20	2	Felt more relaxed

Stress Identification Table:

Complete the stress identification table; this tool will help you effectively pinpoint and manage current stressors. List what's stressing you out, rate your stress level on the Stress-O-Meter scale, and jot down ideas to address each stressor. Additionally, begin to document

which techniques from this workbook you've employed for each stressor, empowering you with a personalized stress management plan.

Stress Identification Table:

What is stressing you out right now?	**How stressed are you on the Stress o meter scale?**	**Ideas to address your stress, including what techniques you have used from this workbook**

EXTRA TOOLS FOR YOUR TOOLBOX TO A CALMER YOU

Within this hackster, you have learned how stress is closely connected to your anxiety and the intricate connection between the two, along with a wealth of insights and practical techniques to manage your issues effectively.

Let's refresh your way to success with the key takeaways you have learned:

Understanding Stress: Good, Bad and Ugly Stress

- Stress is like a pressure cooker. It can be both beneficial (Eustress) and harmful (Bad or Ugly stress). Eustress can motivate and enhance performance, but bad stress can lead to unhealthy coping patterns.
- Bad stress, when it lingers and becomes chronic, often results in negative health outcomes such as anxiety, irritability, headaches or intestinal issues.
- Ugly stress can cause severe health issues, including trouble sleeping, high blood pressure, and weight gain.

How stress is linked to your anxiety

- Stress is in everyone's life, and it's like an ignition switch for anxiety. As you have learned, the link between stress and anxiety is crucial to understand for effective management of both. This is a secret weapon in managing these emotional states.
- Learning how to handle stress effectively is key since it’s impossible to avoid it altogether. So managing your stress will help to reduce its impact on anxiety.

The nervous system and Anxiety

- Anxiety isn’t hardwired. It often develops over time due to the brain misreading everyday experiences as dangerous.
- Understanding the sympathetic (stress triggering) and parasympathetic (calming) nervous system is super crucial for controlling your anxiety and stress effectively.

The Sympathetic Nervous System and Anxiety

- The sympathetic nervous system is like a gas pedal in a car, pushing the body into a fight or flight response when reacting to stressors.
- Non-life-threatening stressors can trigger the fight or flight response, which then leads to anxiety as the stress hormones like cortisol are released into the body.

The Parasympathetic Nervous system and the Calm you.

- The parasympathetic nervous system acts as the brakes in a car, slowing the stress response and flooding the body with calmness.

- Activating the parasympathetic nervous system brings relaxation, reduces tension, slows your breathing, lowers your heart rate and creates a peaceful state of mind and body.

Managing Your Stress with the Stress O Meter

- The Stress O Meter is a valuable tool for gauging your daily stress levels on a scale from 0 to 10. Therefore, you can easily track your stress over time.
- You have learned the “Breathe, Not Seethe Technique," a practical, powerful method for reducing stress and calming your anxiety by connecting to your parasympathetic nervous system, thereby gaining control of your stress and anxiety levels.

The “For Your Eyes Only Technique”

- The “For Your Eyes Only Technique” is a thought-stopping approach to help manage anxious thoughts and feelings caused by stress.
- Remember, this technique is so powerful and can be discreetly used in public to alleviate your anxiety.

Identifying Stress Triggers

- By identifying your own stress triggers, you have learned practical ideas to address your stress triggers, such as creating boundaries, managing time effectively and practicing stress reduction techniques, which can reduce overall stress and improve your well-being.

"You don't have to control your thoughts.
You just have to stop letting them control you" - Dan Millman

Review and Reflection:

Engage with these questions to deepen your insights from this hackster. Uncover the valuable lessons you've learned and strategize how to apply them to your journey toward a more serene version of yourself. Your understanding is the key to unlocking lasting calmness.

Understanding Stress: Good, Bad and Ugly Stress

Can you identify a recent experience when bad stress negatively affected an experience?

____

____

What were your coping mechanisms, and how effective were they?

____

____

Have you experienced "ugly stress" where chronic stress led to severe health issues or emotional challenges?

____

____

What strategies did you use to reduce your stress levels?

____

____

How Stress Connects to Your Anxiety

Think of a recent stressful event in your life. Did this stress trigger anxiety?

____

____

How did you deal with both stress and anxiety in that situation?

____

____

Can you identify a stress-related trigger that often leads to anxiety? How do you plan to address or manage this trigger in the future?

____

____

The Nervous System and anxiety

How aware are you of your anxiety loop? Can you think of a recurring thought or feeling that often arises when you feel anxious? What are they?

____

____

Thinking of your own experiences, have you ever perceived non-threatening situations as dangerous due to your anxiety?

____

____

What were the outcomes of these situations?

____

____

The Sympathetic Nervous System and Anxiety

Think of a recent situation where you felt your body's fight or flight response, your sympathetic nervous system active due to stress. How did this affect your feelings and actions?

____

____

Consider experiences where the fight or flight response unnecessarily escalated your stress. What techniques can you introduce to prevent these responses?

____

____

The Parasympathetic Nervous System and the Calm you

Thinking about the last time you experienced a deep calmness. How did you connect to your parasympathetic nervous system to access this state?

____

____

In what different ways can you create habits to activate your parasympathetic nervous system more consistently to reduce your anxiety and create calmness in your life?

____

____

Managing Stress with the Stress O Meter

Having used the Stress-O-Meter to gauge your stress levels. How has this tool improved your self-awareness and stress patterns?

____

____

Are you keeping a log of your stress levels and stress reduction techniques? What improvements have you noticed since you started using these tools?

____

____

The "For Your Eyes Only Technique"

- Have you tried the "For Your Eyes Only Technique"? If so, when and where did you use it?

- What feelings were you experiencing before and after using this technique?

- List three times throughout your daily routine when you can make this a habit for effectively managing your stress and anxiety.

Identifying Stress Triggers:

- Think about a specific stress trigger that has recently affected you. How have you addressed this trigger, and what were the results?

- Are there stress triggers you haven't addressed yet? How do you plan to tackle them to reduce stress and improve your overall well-being?

Hackster 2: And Finally:

As we conclude Hackster 2, our journey into understanding stress, we've explored the nuances of stress and its connection to anxiety and dissected the nervous system's workings. But here's the catch – we're just getting started. Hackster 3 awaits, where we'll dive deeper into practical techniques.

"The more you believe in your own ability to succeed, the more likely it is that you will" - **Shawn Achor**

HACKSTER 3
CHANGE YOUR THOUGHT, CHANGE YOUR MIND

"It's not whether you get knocked down, it's whether you get up" - Vince Lombardi

What You'll Learn in Hackster 3:

In Hackster 3, you will further your journey to mastering your thoughts and emotions. We will dive into proven practical techniques and insights that will empower you to reshape your inner landscape, moving from anxiety to calmness and negativity to positivity. Let's continue building the foundation for a more balanced and peaceful mindset.

Here's a sneak peek of what else lies ahead:

Mastering Your Thoughts and Feelings – A foundation

Understanding your irrational thoughts:

- Begin by delving into the world of irrational thoughts and how they often operate automatically influenced by your emotions. This learning lays the groundwork for recognizing and managing thought patterns, leading to a more positive and balanced mental state.

Listening to Your Thoughts:

- As you walk along this journey, start by learning how to listen to your thoughts and recognize their profound impact on your feelings and experiences. Understand that many of these thoughts serve no useful purpose and that persistent anxious thoughts often swamp your mind.

Tracking Your Negative Thoughts:

- Develop the skill of tracking your negative self-chitter-chatter and identifying recurring patterns in your thoughts. This fundamental skill empowers you to work actively on transforming these patterns, ultimately reducing your anxiety and stress.

Shifting to Positive Thoughts:

- Lay the found work for a shift from negative to positive thoughts. Recognize the substantial benefits of powerful change, but also acknowledge it requires time and effort to reshape your patterns.

The "Shrink and Blink Technique"

- Begin by exploring the power of the "Shrink and Blink Technique" as a fantastic tool for swiftly reducing negative thoughts, anxiety and stress.

Identifying anxiety Triggers:

- Unravel your personal anxiety triggers, providing you with the foresight to manage situations that previously led to anxiety. Gain insight into how your internal dialogue influences your emotional state, allowing you to regain control over your thoughts and feelings.

Replacing Triggers with Positive Images

- Recognize the transformative potential of replacing specific anxiety triggers with positive mental images. This shift enables you to respond differently to your triggers.

The "Instant Trigger Change Technique"

- Learning this technique will facilitate the rapid replacement of negative triggers with positive mental images, leaving you feeling calm and relaxed.

The "Thought Stopping Technique"

- Diving in and learning the steps of the "Thought Stopping Technique" will be a powerful technique to interrupt your anxious thought patterns and replace them with positive, empowering ones.

So, are you ready to deepen your understanding of the busy chitter chatter free flowing in your mind…

let's go…

Serene Breaths Unleashed: Dive into tranquility with Hackster 3's signature technique!

Become the master of tranquillity with Box Breathing:

Box breathing, also known as square breathing, is an accessible breathing exercise designed to alleviate stress and anxiety.

Prepare for serenity:

Begin by finding a quiet environment where you can concentrate on your breathing without distractions.

As you practice this technique, visualize a box with four even sides. With each step, imagine you are following one side of a box. Start at the top corner and work your way around the edge of the box until you've returned to the starting point.

Inhale Slowly for a Count of 4:

Take deliberate and unhurried inhalation, counting to 4 as you fill your lungs with air.

Hold your breath for a count of 4:

Calmly hold your breath for a steady count of 4, embracing the pause in your breathing.

Exhale Gradually for a Count of 4:

Release tension by exhaling slowly and steadily, counting to 4 as you let go of your breath.

Wait for a count of 4 and Repeat:

Embrace the rhythm of box breathing by pausing for a count of 4 after each time you exhale.

Repeat this cycle to deepen your relaxation.

Adjusting for Comfort:

If 4 seconds feels challenging initially, start with a 2-second count until you find your comfort zone.

The box breathing technique gradually slows your breathing, fostering a heightened sense of calm throughout your entire body.

Unlock the potential of bx breathing – it is such a simple yet impactful practice to weave tranquility into your daily routine.

Controlled breathing influences your brain's neurotransmitters like serotonin (the happy hormone), contributing to a relaxed, calm mood

MASTERING YOUR THOUGHTS AND FEELINGS – A FOUNDATION

To think or not to think – that is the question.

But if only we had a choice only to think positive thoughts, life would be great.

These irrational, anxious thoughts are just there, bubbling in the background. Most of the time, we aren't always conscious of them, as we never usually pay attention to our thoughts. Therefore, they can become judgmental and self-critical, and we tend to believe our thoughts are factual.

This bubbling cauldron of automatic thoughts is your interpretation of what's happening around you rather than actual facts. They depend on what life is like for you right now.

- If you're happy and feel good about yourself, your thoughts will indicate this and be positive and encouraging.
- If you're feeling low and sad, your thoughts will show this, and you will be gloomy and unenthusiastic.

Many of our thoughts and feelings are undeniably valid. It's OKAY to feel:

- Angry when the wifi drops out just as you are about to send an important email,
- Sad if someone said something hurtful about you or
- Frustrated when you get comfy in bed and realize you forgot to take off your toupee.

Our automatic survival mechanism

As I mentioned, our automatic survival mechanism that once protected our ancestors from such danger and threat to fight off a saber-toothed tiger explains why our brains are wired to favor negative thoughts and feelings in a fearful situation. Focusing on the worst-case scenario was then our primary way to survive.

Life is so different now, and unfortunately, with the external build-up of daily stressors, anxiety increases and boom! There we are in the depths of the deep, dark well, trying to tread water. Therefore, we need to begin to change the way we think consciously.

Yes, that sounds great, but the first step in changing our thoughts is to be aware of our negative thoughts and then consciously change and reword them.

Tune in: When you start to listen to your thoughts, you will be surprised to find most of them are useless, unimportant chitter-chatter that flips and flaps through your mind at the speed of light.

The National Science Foundation estimates that:

THOUGHT STATISTICS	NUMBERS
Total Daily Thoughts (Per person)	12,000 to 60,000 thoughts per day
Negative Thoughts (Percentage)	80% of daily thoughts are negative thoughts
Recurring Thoughts (Percentage)	95% of daily thoughts are the same thoughts we had yesterday and the day before

So, if you repeatedly think of those anxious thoughts, you will think anxious, negative thoughts far more often than happy ones.

With this shocking revelation, what chance do we have to break this anxious cycle unless we consciously decide to change our thoughts to positive thoughts? https://www.nsf.gov/

So, if you have a busy mind with approximately 60,000 thoughts per day and 80 percent of these thoughts are negative, then you can see how easy it is to fire up your anxiety

What about "your" thoughts?

Are "your" thoughts unhelpful, wondering thoughts that could be:

- Repeating what someone said to you,
- Consistently questioning yourself and coming up with unhelpful answers, or
- Too much rabbiting nonsensical gibber churning through your thoughts and maybe some that you are unaware of.

By tuning into your busy thoughts, you can choose whether to listen to them or NOT.

"Life is what happens when you're busy making other plans" - **John Lennon**

Do you have irrational thinking patterns that trigger your anxiety?

Here are a few of the common, irrational thought patterns to help you understand your complicated patterns of thought:

Irrational Thinking Patterns	**Description**	**Examples**	**Reality Checker**
All-or-nothing thinking	This type of thinking is also called black-and-white thinking, with no gray areas in between, leaving you feeling stuck with no focus on your future	You forgot your friend's birthday, feel like a loser, and are the stupidest, most forgetful person in the world	Understand life is not defined by extremes. There will be alternative options
"Should" thinking	If you think you "should," "ought to," "have to," or "must do" things, this leads to unrealistic pressure on yourself	"I should be in control of my life all the time"	It's time to learn to recognize this thinking pattern and let go of control in certain areas of your life
Catastrophic Thinking	You assume the worst will happen, which includes "what if" questions	If you struggle with health anxiety and notice a freckle on your arm, you may think to yourself, "It's something sinister. What if it's cancer?"	Begin challenging these thoughts with evidence. If it changes shape or color, see your doctor; the odds are it's just an ordinary freckle
Focusing on the Negative	Worrying excessively. Ruminating over negative thoughts while filtering out positive ones	"I have to give a presentation. Everyone will think how bad I am at public speaking, how nervous I am, and it will be a disaster"	Think of the encouraging times you have made presentations and the positive feedback. Realize your audience may not be as critical as you imagine
Wild Irrational Thoughts	Negative beliefs like "I am worthless" or "This always happens to me"	"It didn't go perfectly; therefore, I failed"	Challenge these thoughts; where is the evidence for thinking this way?
Overgeneralizing	When you decide things are worse than they really are. It's when we come to very broad and distorted conclusions	"I am such a bad parent for shouting at the kids"	Break these thoughts down and focus on how to change the situation positively

Let's begin to identify which type of negative thoughts you often have, so it's time to think about what you're thinking.

Keeping a diary or a journal of your thoughts is one of the best ways to become aware of your negative self-talk. Or complete the irrational thinking patterns table.

Try to group these thoughts by theme after a while or by the end of each week.

So, all thoughts about "always" or "never" go together. For example, "I always miss important meetings," "I never say smart things," or "Nobody appreciates me."

This exercise will help you identify which thoughts repeat and which cause greater distress.

Write down the most prominent thoughts you have throughout the day. When you do this, steer clear of ruminating on the thought; instead, write down exactly what the trigger was and the thoughts, feelings and images that come forward.

IRRATIONAL THINKING PATTERNS TABLE

The Thought	Trigger	Emotional and Physical Feelings	Images
Example: "I must do everything perfectly"	Struggled to complete a task	Stress, anxiety, self-criticism	An image of unfinished tasks piling up

IT'S TIME TO BITE BACK! WITH ALTERNATIVE HEALTHY THOUGHTS

Keeping a diary or a journal of your thoughts is one of the best ways to become aware of your negative self-talk.

In Hackster 1, you have already begun to listen up for your negative thoughts and have written these in your diary. So, let's step this up and add another column in your diary or journal. Think of an alternative healthy thought to replace the old continuous negative chitter-chatter. Here's how you are going to do this:

1. Complete the Alternative Healthy Thoughts Log by writing down any harmful, unhelpful thoughts you had during the day to create some distance from your rabbiting inner critic. Observing those thoughts teaches you how to bite back at them, but not literally unless you are hungry!
2. The next step is to write down a helpful thought to replace the unhelpful one.

Check out the examples of anxious, negative thoughts and their positive replacement to give you ideas for transforming these challenging mental patterns

Replacement positive thought examples:

ANXIOUS, NEGATIVE THOUGHT	REPLACEMENT POSITIVE THOUGHT
I can't do this	I can learn to do this
I'm the worst person in the world	I have many good qualities
No one likes me	List the names of your loved ones
I'm not good enough	I am good enough
I'm a failure	Everyone makes mistakes, and I can learn from them
I am hopeless at this	I can learn how to do this

Alternative Healthy Thoughts Log:

DATE AND TIME	YOUR TRIGGERS (WHAT INCREASES THE ANXIETY)	SYMPTOMS (EMOTIONAL & PHYSICAL IN THE BODY?)	NEGATIVE THOUGHTS/IMAGES	REPLACEMENT POSITIVE THOUGHT	OUTCOME (WHAT HAPPENED AS A CONSEQUENCE?)	WHAT YOU COULD DO DIFFERENTLY NEXT TIME YOU HAVE ANXIETY	RATE ON A SCALE FROM 0 TO 10

Grab your Post-It notes, write your replacement positive words on these, and post them in your loo, bathroom, mirror, car, and even the tip of your nose. Keep reminding yourself of the direction you plan to go.

TECHNIQUE: THE "SHRINK AND BLINK TECHNIQUE"

One superb technique to reduce negative thoughts and images is introducing calmness into your life with the "Shrink and Blink Technique."

When you're aware of a painful thought and image, this is a simple yet super powerful way to work with your imagination and thoughts to free you from them.

Step	Description
1.	Think about a negative thought and the image connected to your anxiety
2.	Now, put a frame around the image and send it off into the distance. Blink it on and off, black and white and super-fast like a strobe light. Notice it is shrinking down into a small picture, like a postage stamp or a single dot
3.	Watch it disappear into oblivion as you do this, and feel your shoulders relax
4.	Take a deep breath through your nose for a count of four. Hold your breath for eight and then breathe out through your mouth for eight. Then do it again. Then, keep doing it whenever complex thoughts pop into your mind

To watch extra videos where I show each technique, join the Bonus Companion Course at: https://anxietyhacks.info/info-step1/

Excellent! So keep blink, blink, blinking.

"The secret of change is to focus all your energy not on fighting the old, but on building the new" – Socrates

ANXIETY TRIGGERS

What the dickens are triggers?

(Just in case you are wondering: "What the Dickens" means, it has nothing to do with our Charles; it came about 200 years before Charles Dickens and is a euphemism for the word devil!)

Your devilish anxiety triggers could be so many things that your brain has learned to believe are dangerous and cause you to feel anxious.

Of course, if something makes you feel anxious, you are likely to avoid the situation to avoid getting anxious. This could be:

- An opportunity at work,
- A fun party you have been invited to, or
- Even everyday errands like just nipping out to the shops.

Your anxiety triggers are anything that sends you into your pattern of anxiety. You would either:

- Say something to yourself,
- Make a picture in your mind, or
- Have a feeling.

(Remember what you learned about submodalities in Hackster 1?)

Think About This NOW...

We don't usually pay attention to it, and it happens in a flash. The thought will be brief; the image will be a quick flash, or the feeling will pop up and could well disappear.

What are common anxiety triggers?

Common anxiety triggers can vary from health issues to personal triggers rooted in past experiences. For example:

Anxiety Trigger	Description
Financial worries	For many, it doesn't matter if they are struggling and completely penniless or have a huge bank balance. Their finances can trigger them to worry, and the anxiety builds up
Stress	As we mentioned in the previous Hackster, chronic stress is a common trigger for long-term anxiety
Health problems	This could be some health diagnosis that is challenging to cope with, like a chronic illness or cancer. Which may bring on anxiety with the huge, overwhelming bundle of feelings that would come up
Social Gathering	Going to an event, whether with strangers, close friends (or even people you don't like!), can trigger anxiety for some, but you are not alone. Many people feel like this, which may be diagnosed as a social anxiety disorder
Conflict	For some, all types of conflict can trigger your anxiety, and this could be with a work colleague, spouse, family member, or even that old-school pal on the Internet can trigger anxiety.
Negative thinking	As I mentioned earlier, our minds are conditioned to think negative thoughts, which can cause anxiety
Caffeine	An overload of caffeine consumption, such as your morning coffee delight, could trigger your anxiety. It can be okay in small doses, but everyone is different, and tolerance levels vary from body to body. Reducing the daily amount of caffeine improves their anxiety, or substituting a decaffeinated delight for caffeinated coffee
Personal triggers	Your personal triggers are often related to a bad memory or traumatic event in your past. These could be conscious or unconscious. This could start with a thought, feeling, something you touch or see, a smell, a song, or even a place. If you were to think of a phrase your mother/father would say when you were young, this could bring up many different emotions

IT IS NOW TIME TO IDENTIFY YOUR SPECIFIC TRIGGERS

How to detect your triggers

What's the very first thing you would do?

You'll have your very own specific triggers. So, what you need to do is begin to identify them. What precisely causes you to go from feeling okay to suddenly thinking or feeling anxious? Do you have any idea right now?

It's time to listen. . . To you.

By spending more time listening to how you're talking to yourself, you have more chances to change these thoughts to more positive, self-empowering ones.

Your triggers could be external and might be:

- **Something you see**, maybe someone was glaring at you at work, or you spotted a spider in the fireplace. Maybe seeing a text on your phone from someone has caused you to feel anxious in the past. It could be anything you SEE.
- **Something you hear**, maybe someone else is talking about a difficult experience with their anxiety. It could be anything you HEAR.
- **Something you touch,** this could be a specific food you touch that you have prepared when you felt anxious in the past. It could be anything you TOUCH.
- **Something you taste**, eating a meal and taking that first bite causes anxious thoughts and feelings for many, especially if you have an eating disorder. It could be anything you TASTE.
- **Something you smell**, tantalizing aromas wafting as you walk past bakers or the smell of someone cooking. It could be anything you SMELL.

Your triggers could be internal or mental and might be:

- **Something you might be thinking** in your head, such as an image of you looking panic-stricken before a presentation or an image of you standing on the scales looking deflated,
- **Something you might be saying to yourself,** such as "I've had such a stressful day, I'll go crazy if I can't stop feeling anxious," or "People will laugh at me if I say anything at this meeting,
- **Something you might feel,** such as hopeless, helpless, lonely, sad, bored, upset, guilty, worthless, etc.

The most important point we can learn here is that the internal triggers that cause your anxious feelings are all in your head; they aren't real!

The busy mind is like a butterfly that flies from one flower to another, never standing still.

"STOP BELIEVING EVERYTHING YOU THINK" — **Kate Hudson-Hall**

If you have a negative thought or you get up in the morning and think: "Arrghhh . . . another day that looks like it's going to be challenging!!!" The chances are it will be. . . we attract negative energy because your mind thinks that's what you want (very clever!). So that's what you get (even cleverer!).

You can begin to change right here; changing these old behaviors into new positive ones is possible.

"An anxious mind resembles a river that rushes over rocks, never finding a moment of stillness"- Kate Hudson-Hall

Questions to ask yourself to help identify what your triggers are.

I want you now to think about what your specific triggers might be. Begin to unravel the pattern of what gets you zipping down into that anxious spiral.

What's the first thing that happens that sends you spiraling down into your anxiety hole?

Questions to ask yourself to help you further identify more details about your anxiety triggers:

To help you further identify your anxiety-ridden triggers, think about a past episode that has you slipping into an anxious spiral.

Answer these questions:

What is the first thing that happens and sends you spiraling down into your anxiety pit? Complete the anxiety trigger table.

Anxiety Trigger Table:

Imagine:	**Your answer**
What do you see?	
What do you hear?	
What do you taste?	
What do you think to yourself?	
What images do you have?	
What do you touch?	
What do you smell?	
What feelings are you having?	

You've identified your triggers; now think of a replacement image.

Before you move on to the "Instant Trigger Change Technique," think of a positive replacement image or movie of you looking and feeling calm and serene to substitute for the trigger image. Complete the replacement image table.

Trigger Image Replacement Table:

YOUR TRIGGERS	REPLACEMENT IMAGE OR MOVIE
1.	
2.	
3.	
4.	
5.	
6.	
7.	
8.	
9.	
10.	

How to change your triggers instantly with the "Instant Trigger Change Technique."

Now you have your list of specific triggers that cause your anxiety and positive replacement images; I will show you how you can learn to change your triggers instantly with this excellent NLP (Neuro Linguist Programming) technique.

Oh, yes, this is where it gets inspiring. In this technique, you'll be replacing the trigger image with your replacement image or movie of yourself engaging in new positive behavior, looking happy and free from your anxiety. Before you begin, read the client example using the "Instant Trigger Change Technique" to see how beneficial it is for changing triggers positively.

Client Example: Using the "Instant Trigger Change Technique" to work with her triggers and reduce anxiety:

Meet Sally. She is a 32-year-old professional who came to see me for help to address her overwhelming anxiety triggered by work overload and other work-related stressors. Her primary triggers included the sound of her work email and the sight of her work desk.

Identifying of Triggers:

In therapy sessions, Sally identified specific triggers that initiated her anxiety to spiral. Just the thought of checking work emails and facing her cluttered desk triggered intense feelings of pressure and looming failure.

Creating Replacement Images:

- Sally created positive replacement images for each trigger as part of our work together. For the work email trigger, she imagined an image of herself confidently managing her emails, feeling organized and in control.
- For the clutter desk trigger, Sally replaced the mental image with one of a neat, organized workspace that conveyed a sense of calmness.

The "Instant Trigger Change Technique":

Starting the Technique:

Sally closed her eyes and focused on the first trigger – checking work emails. She vividly imagined the scene, including the familiar ping of the email notification.

Blanking out the Trigger Image:

Sally immediately transformed the vivid screen into a blank white screen. This step was crucial in disrupting the automatic anxiety response connected with the trigger.

Inserting the Replacement Image:

Sally swiftly replaced the blank screen with the positive image she had crafted – an image of herself efficiently and confidently managing work email. I then encouraged her to engage all her senses in this visualization, making it as vivid and detailed as possible.

Repetition and Reinforcement:

I then guided Sally through this process multiple times, allowing her to experience the replacement image each time she thought about checking work emails. Repetition was key in reinforcing the new association between the trigger and the positive image.

The Outcome:

After several repetitions, Sally noticed a shift in her emotional response. The once anxiety-inducing trigger of checking work emails became associated with a sense of control and confidence. She no longer felt the immediate surge and dread the trigger had previously brought up.

We then worked on the trigger for her cluttered desk image.

Conclusion:

Sally's journey is a fine example of how powerful the "Instant Trigger Change Technique" can be. By changing how her brain connects anxiety triggers, she took control of how she felt. Because Sally kept practicing, her work-related anxiety went down massively. This story highlights how flexible and beneficial NLP techniques can be in helping you take charge and change how you feel inside.

Now it is your turn to change how YOU feel inside with your triggers.

TECHNIQUE: THE "INSTANT TRIGGER CHANGE TECHNIQUE"

So, find a quiet place and sit down. I want you to take each trigger you have identified and follow the instructions below.

Read through all the steps to know where you're going with this.

The "Instant Trigger Change Technique" Steps:

1.	Think about your first trigger that sends you down into your negative pattern of anxiety. It could be an image of you standing in your kitchen and you hear your cell phone ring.
2.	Imagine a movie starting from this point and immediately white it out, making the movie screen completely blank—white.
3.	Replace the image immediately with an image or a movie of yourself engaging in a new positive behavior, looking happy and being free from your anxiety. To do this, imagine you are swiping to the next photo in your gallery on your phone. Just flipping that old trigger image to a powerful, positive image, such as an image or movie of you walking tall in a park or on a beach, feeling calmer and more positive about yourself. It will allow you to attach the trigger to the thought of you being free from the pattern.
4.	Repeat Steps 1 - 3 a few times on the first trigger and notice yourself thinking differently about that trigger.

To watch extra videos where I show each technique, join the Bonus Companion Course at: https://anxietyhacks.info/info-

Test: Can you snigger without your trigger?
If not, keep working through all your triggers that spring to the surface and break this pattern as you link this old trigger to a positive new image.

READY TO BAT YOUR DIFFICULT THOUGHTS OUT OF THE PARK?

Here is an example of a client who had a challenging experience traveling in Thailand that sent her down into the depths of anxiety and panic attacks.

Trekking across Thailand on her own had been a particularly stressful experience when she caught a stomach virus while traveling.

She said, "I was ready to explode. I just couldn't hold it. Having to stop the bus for the fourth time, I flew from the bus, dove into the wooden shack called a bathroom, and let go. The door flew open, and I could only see groping eyes from the bus." Humiliation was an understatement.

From then on, whenever traveling anywhere, even back home in the United Kingdom, whether by car, train, plane, or donkey, the thoughts and feelings of being trapped and suffocating were overwhelming. Her anxiety would detonate, and her panic attacks would erupt.

Several different tools and techniques that I teach you helped my client, and one of them was the "Thought-Stopping Technique." Whenever she was aware of her triggering thoughts that led to her anxiety rising, she used this technique to stop those thoughts dead in their tracks by redirecting her attention from the destructive, repetitive thought patterns. It is simple but brings a sense of calmness.

"Believe you can, and you're halfway there." - Theodore Roosevelt

TECHNIQUE: THE "THOUGHT-STOPPING TECHNIQUE"

So, to reduce your anxiety and the mumbling mutterings looping through your supersonic brain, I will teach you this effective tool called the "Thought-Stopping Technique."

It is a technique for stopping and challenging that anxious beastly dialog and the escalating emotional whirlwind of increasing negative feelings with a "stop" command, giving you a sense of control. You're breaking the harmful thought habit and reinforcing a sense of reassurance.

Why does it work?

Why thought stopping works is pretty straightforward; you interrupt the beastly mutterings with a "stop" command as a reminder and distraction.

As I have mentioned (if you didn't skip over that page!), usually, your obsessive thoughts tend to repeat in your mind. Left unchecked, they become automatic in a never-ending cycle of spiraling disaster. When using the thought-stopping technique, you become aware of the damaging thought chains and redirect your attention away from harmful, repetitive thought habits.

Thought-stopping requires consistent motivation and doesn't work on multiple negative, anxious thoughts at a time.

You've identified more of a pattern of your painful thoughts that intensifies your anxiety earlier in this Hackster. Now, you'll learn the steps to stop these beastly thoughts.

Step	Description
1.	**Notice the thought.** Close your eyes and imagine a situation in which an anxious thought/feeling may occur.
2.	**Thought Interruption.** Set a timer for two minutes. Close your eyes and ponder on your anxious thought. When you hear the ring, shout, "Stop!" then "Get lost!" or "Puff off" in whatever terminology you wish! Maybe stronger words might be more powerful for you. I know what I use!
	Imagine a giant stop sign in your head if you're the visual type. You could also have a loose rubber band on your wrist to snap at this point. You could snap your fingers or even pinch yourself if you don't have one.
	Now, empty your mind of all but the calm and non-anxious thoughts and reroute your mind to an inspiring or distracting thought. So, rather than your obsessive thought, make up some positive statements and images appropriate for the target situation.
	A rerouting thought might be a saying that encourages you or an empowering or relaxing memory.
	Set a goal of about thirty seconds after the stop.
	If the distressing thought returns during that time, shout, "Stop!" swiping away the evil leprechaun from your shoulder and, "Get lost," snapping your rubber band or your fingers.
3.	**Now, do this without the timer.** Now, take control of the beastly anxious whispering without the timer. While pondering the unwanted thought, shout, "Stop!" and "Get lost," then bring up the giant stop sign and snap your rubber band or pinch yourself.
	When you succeed in stopping the thought on several occasions with the shouted command, begin interrupting the thought with a "Stop!" and "Get lost" in a usual voice.
	After succeeding in stopping the thought by using your normal speaking voice, start interrupting the thought with "Stop!" and "Get lost" in a whisper.
	When the whisper completely interrupts your stressful thoughts, imagine hearing "Stop!" and "Get lost" shouted inside your mind.
	When you can achieve this successfully, you can stop thoughts alone or in public without anyone knowing what you're doing.

To watch extra videos where I show each technique,
join the Bonus Companion Course at: https://anxietyhacks.info/info-step1/

Excellent! Changing your thoughts will take time, so I want you to practice thought-stopping every day as many times as possible—all day. Over time, you'll be able to stop unwanted thoughts immediately.

The "Thought Stopping Technique" Tracker

Use this table to track the situations or locations where you could or have used the "Thought Stopping Technique" connected with your anxious thoughts and patterns over time.

The "Thought Stopping Technique" Tracker:

Date/Time	Situation/Location	Triggering Thought	Thought Stopping Action
Example	On public transport	"I feel trapped"	I shouted "Stop" in my head and "Get Lost" and focused on a past successful journey

EXTRA TOOLS FOR YOUR TOOLBOX TO A CALMER YOU

In this Hackster, you have learned to recognize and challenge negative thought patterns and triggers, ultimately promoting a more positive and calm mindset.

Let's refresh your way to success with the key takeaways you have learned:

Understanding Your Irrational Thoughts:

- You now understand your feelings often automatically influence your thoughts.
- This knowledge helps you recognize and control your thought patterns, promoting a more positive and balanced mind.

Listening to Your Thoughts

- By tuning in to your thoughts, you've learned how they can shape your feelings and experiences.
- While listening to your thoughts, you now understand how often they serve no useful purpose, and frequently persistent anxious thoughts can swarm your mind.

Tracking Your Negative Thoughts

- You have learned to develop the skill of tracking negative self-talk and identifying recurring patterns in your thoughts.
- By recognizing these thought patterns, you can actively work on changing them and reducing anxiety and stress.

Shifting to Positive thoughts

- There are huge benefits to changing negative thoughts into positive alternatives to counter harmful self-talk to improve your mental well-being.
- Understand it takes time and effort to change your thought patterns.

The "Shrink and Blink Technique"

- Using this technique to reduce negative thoughts, you can quickly reduce anxiety and stress and build on a sense of inner peace.
- Applying deep breathing will also further promote relaxation, and by continuously practicing this technique, you will maintain a calmer mindset.

Identifying Anxiety Triggers

- Having now identified your personal anxiety triggers will allow you to anticipate and manage situations that could have led to anxiety in the past.
- Understanding how your internal dialogue influences your anxiety can help you regain control over the way you think and feel.

Replacing Triggers with Positive Images

- You have learned the huge benefits of replacing your specific trigger image with new positive ones.
- Replacing anxiety triggers with positive images allows you to react differently to your triggers, creating a more relaxed and confident approach.

The "Instant Trigger Change Technique"

- Using the "Instant Trigger Change Technique," you can quickly replace negative triggers with positive mental images to make you calmer.
- Practicing this technique frequently will empower you to take control of your thoughts.

The "Thought Stopping Technique"

- Using the "Thought Stopping Technique" interrupts anxious thought patterns and replaces them with more positive, empowering ones, leading you into peace and calmness without all the nonsensical chitter-chatter.
- Of course, over time, you'll stop these thoughts immediately, so consistent practice is essential for success at reducing your anxiety and giving you a greater sense of control.

"The greatest glory in living lies not in never falling, but in rising every time we fall" - **Nelson Mandela**

Review and Reflection:

Dive into these questions and unlock the treasure trove of insights you've gained in this Hackster. Discover what you've learned and how these powerful tools can sculpt a version of you that's calmer, stronger and ready to continue conquering anxiety.

Understanding Irrational Thoughts:

Have you noticed moments when your thoughts seem automatic and negative? What were you thinking about, and how did it make you feel?

Are you paying enough attention to your thought patterns? By paying more attention to what you are telling yourself, how might this benefit your efforts to overcome anxiety?

____

____

Write down how and where you could set up reminders to help you tune into what you tell yourself that makes you anxious.

____

____

Listening to your thoughts:

What are further ways you could become more conscious of your negative thoughts? What strategies can you use to catch these thoughts as they pop into your head?

____

____

How can actively listening to your thoughts lead to more positive outcomes in your everyday life and reduce your anxiety?

____

____

Tracking your negative thoughts:

Have you noticed recurring thought patterns in your diary or journal? What patterns have you become aware of, and how do they relate to your anxiety?

____

____

Once you recognize your negative thought patterns, what will you do to start to reduce these and, therefore, reduce your anxiety?

____

____

Shifting to Positive thoughts

Are you practicing the skill of changing negative thoughts into positive alternatives? Write down an example of how this has improved your mindset.

____

____

What steps can you take to make shifting to positive thoughts a consistent and effective part of your everyday life?

____

____

The "Shrink and Blink Techniques"

How did the "Shrink and Blink Technique" affect your anxiety levels?

____

____

How can you incorporate the "Shrink and Blink Technique" into your daily routine and in what situations do you see yourself applying this technique most effectively to maintain a calmer you?

____

____

Identifying Anxiety Triggers

Can you identify specific triggers that consistently create anxiety in your life, such as stress, financial worries or work situations?

____

____

What strategies or techniques can you implement to handle these identified triggers that reduce their impact on your mental well-being?

____

____

Replacing Triggers with Positive Images

Have you begun to replace your anxiety triggers with empowering and positive mental scenarios? What impact has this had on your triggers?

____

____

How can you reinforce the idea that your mind can be retrained to react differently to triggers and bring about calmness from within?

____

____

The "Instant Trigger Change Technique":

How do you feel when you successfully take control of your thoughts using the "Instant Trigger Change Technique"? What areas of your life do you believe will have the most impact?

____

____

List three ways to ensure this technique becomes a reliable and empowering tool in your daily efforts to overcome anxiety.

____

____

The "Thought Stopping Technique"

How has the "Thought Stopping Technique" helped you regain control and calmness?

____

____

In what situations do you find thought-stopping most valuable? List three ways you could use this technique that you haven't already.

____

____

Hackster 3: And Finally:

As we wrap up the transformative journey of Hackster 3, let's dive into your next adventure and enrich your journey toward a calmer and more mindful you. Get ready to surf without water in Hackster 4.

"Worrying does not take away tomorrow's troubles. It takes away today's peace" - **Randy Armstrong**

HACKSTER 4

LEARN TO SURF WITHOUT WATER!

"Believe you can, and you're halfway there" - Theodore Roosevelt

What You'll Learn in Hackster 4:

To take the next leap in your self-discovery journey, in Hackster 4, we're unraveling the complexities between feelings and emotions, giving you a deeper insight into these often mixed-up concepts. So, join me in exploring a more centered and emotionally empowered you. Let's keep this transformative journey rolling.

Here's a sneak peek of what else lies ahead:

Understanding Feelings and Emotions:

Our journey begins with exploring emotions and feelings and understanding the difference between emotions and feelings, two terms often used interchangeably. We'll explore how:

- Emotions are primarily physical sensations and automatic reactions, and
- Feelings are mental associations, conscious and deeply connected to your emotional experiences.

The consequences of suppressing feelings:

- We'll be learning what happens when you avoid or hide feelings and
- Learn how this can lead to various psychological and physical issues, including anxiety, anger, addiction and more, affecting our mental and physical well-being.

Mindfulness as a solution:

- Discovering mindfulness as a practical solution to address the challenges of neglected feelings and
- Explore the power of mindfulness to help you stay present, increase emotional awareness and unlock numerous benefits.

How to benefit from practicing mindfulness:

- Acquiring the incredible skills to practice both informal and formal mindfulness, offering techniques for increased presence in daily life, and
- Learning how these mindfulness practices can effectively reduce anxiety.

Serene Breaths Unleashed: Dive into tranquility with Hackster 4's signature technique!

Unlock the Power of Deep Breathing for Anxiety Relief

Deep breathing helps to relieve shortness of breath by preventing air from getting trapped in your lungs and allowing you to breathe in fresher air. It lowers resting blood pressure, reduces stress and anxiety and relieves pain.

Variety of Names, One Powerful Technique:

Deep breathing, also known as diaphragmatic, abdominal, or belly breath, involves thoroughly filling your lungs.

The unnatural Perception:

Deep breathing may feel unnatural for many due to societal influences on body image. The cultural preference for a flat stomach leads people to hold their stomach muscles, which causes shallow breathing or chest breathing, which becomes their normal way of breathing. Which then increases tension and anxiety.

Shallow Breathing's Impact:

Shallow breathing restricts the diaphragm's range of movement, limiting the lower lung's access to oxygenated air, which can result in feelings of heightened anxiety or breathlessness.

The Power of Deep Abdominal Breathing:

Embrace deep abdominal breathing for full oxygen exchange. This process enables the valuable exchange of oxygen coming in, for outgoing carbon dioxide, leading to a slowed heartbeat and lowered blood pressure.

Focus your Breath to Help Concentration:

Use your breath to help focus your attention on slow, deep breathing while disengaging from distracting thoughts and sensations.

Prepare for Serenity:

Find a quiet, comfortable space to sit or lie down. Begin with a normal breath, then transition to a deep breath. Inhale slowly through your nose, allowing your chest and lower belly to rise as you fill your lungs. Let your abdomen fully expand. Exhale slowly through your mouth or nose, whichever feels more natural.

Practice makes Perfect:

Once you've mastered the basics, progress to regular sessions of controlled breathing. For this type of breathing to become automatic, you'll need to practice it daily. Try doing the exercise three or four times daily for up to 10 minutes.

Unlock the potential of deep breathing as a powerful tool for anxiety relief. Embrace the journey toward calmness and mindfulness with these simple yet effective steps.

Research found that taking at least ten consecutive diaphragmatic breaths twice a day for two weeks significantly reduced anxiety (Chen, 2017). https://onlinelibrary.wiley.com/doi/abs/10.1111/ppc.12184

Deep breathing lowers cortisol levels (the stress hormone), reducing stress's impact on the body and mind.

Are you ready to dive into this fascinating world of emotions, feelings and mindfulness? Let's get exploring…

UNDERSTANDING YOUR FEELINGS AND EMOTIONS

What is the difference between feelings and emotions?

First, let's understand the difference between your feelings and emotions as they are often used interchangeably, and there is a close connection between them.

What are emotions?

Your emotions are:

- Solely physical bodily sensations,
- The automatic reactions the body has to certain stimuli (for example, the sadness we feel when we lose a loved one),
- Your nervous system's electrical, chemical, and hormonal releases and
- Not conscious and arise from the unconscious.

An emotional reaction happens if we are afraid or fearful of something. Our heart starts pounding, we tense up, our mouth becomes dry, our muscles contract, and we sweat.

The most common emotions:

- Anxiousness
- Happiness
- Sadness
- Anger
- Fear
- Disgust
- Embarrassment

YOUR EMOTIONS ARE PHYSICAL STATES,

WHEREAS FEELINGS ARE MENTAL ASSOCIATIONS

What are feelings? Your feelings:

- Are reactions to your emotions,
- Come up when your brain assigns a meaning to the emotional experience you are having,
- Are conscious, and they spring to life after you become aware in your brain of the physical changes in your body, which allows you to experience the happiness and sadness in life with its ups and downs and
- They can become even more specific than an emotional response, although they can also spring up from your physical reactions to numerous things.

Here is a list of emotions and feelings that could arise connected to each emotion:

Emotion and Feelings Example Table:

EMOTION	FEELINGS
Anxious	Stressed, Worried, Nervous, Cautious, and Afraid
Happiness	Confident, Excited, Relaxed, Thankful, and Confident
Sadness	Tearful, Disappointed, Regretful, Disillusioned, and Depressed
Anger	Annoyed, Grumpy, Offended, Frustrated, and Disgusted
Fear	Frightened, Threatened, Scared, Nervous, and Unsafe
Disgust	Abused, Revolted, Guilt, Jealousy, and Betrayal
Embarrassed	Pathetic, Guilty, Lonely, Confused, and Self-conscious
Hurt	Abandoned, Jealous, Betrayed, Deprived, and Isolated

The American Psychological Association (APA) explains anxiety as an emotion exhibited by feelings of tension, worried thoughts, and physical changes like increased blood pressure. Anxiety—APA. https://www.apa.org/topics/anxiety/

"People who wonder whether the glass is half empty or half full are missing the point. The glass is refillable" – Simon Sinek

Although emotions might not remain as long as feelings, your emotions trigger feelings, and your feelings trigger more emotions!

Off we go on a never-ending emotional-feeling loop!

Your specific anxious feelings could set off a never-ending loop of challenging and confusing emotions and feelings. But it all happens in a flash, and before we know it, we are a tightly wrapped coil of anxiety.

BUT... WERE YOU EVER TAUGHT WHAT TO DO WHEN YOU EXPERIENCE EXPLODING EMOTIONS AND FEELINGS?

What do you do when you experience overwhelming feelings? Do you express them somehow, or do you just push them aside?

Turn on those listening ears now; if you are not beneficially expressing your feelings, it can lead to many health issues.

Most of my clients were taught:

- To ignore and suppress their naturally stirring feelings from a young age. Maybe their mother would tell them, "Stop crying and pull yourself together," or peers would tease them, calling them "A cry-baby," or ridicule them for showing their emotions.
- That the feelings they had were terrible or made them a bad person.

If this is the case for you, you have probably learned to ignore them, or if you have a big enough broom, you sweep them under the carpet.

According to new research, experiencing and accepting feelings is critical to our mental health.

Do your feelings have superpowers?

Our feelings are super powerful. Sometimes, it's as if they have their own superpowers!

If you deny them, those darn feelings have to come out somehow. They need to be expressed and eventually claw their way to the surface in unhealthy and harmful ways.

Allow yourself to feel.

Keeping your emotions and feelings squashed down inside will only end in disaster. Allow yourself to feel those darn feelings. You will be so much more genuinely calm. And that authentic you can begin to shine.

So, what happens to the emotions and feelings if they are not expressed?

Oh yes, they lurk there deep within, manifesting, bubbling away, and with a build-up of further difficult experiences linked to painful emotions and the beastly feelings. They all have to be released in some way. Which for some may be having a migraine every time you're stressed, or for others, reaching out for alcohol or drugs. For others, it could be other forms of self-harm.

But for me, it came out in...

developing an eating disorder for fifteen years.

The consequences of denied feelings

The consequences of feelings you have denied or suppressed for such a long time could explode into:

- Anxiety and fears
- Anger
- Addiction
- Eating Disorders
- Difficulty experiencing healthy relationships
- Low self-esteem, shame, or guilt. For example:

I had a very emotional client who came to see me. She had lost her sister fifteen years previously. When her sister died, her parents pressured her to move on with her life. So, she did just that and "got on with it."

Now, fifteen years later, she felt she couldn't continue. Her unexpressed emotions and feelings about her sister's passing had boiled to the surface. One day, she found herself crying and thinking about her sister's death fifteen years earlier. The same thing happened the next day and the day after; she was constantly thinking of her sister's death and crying.

After discussing this with my client, she finally understood she was crying the tears she had suppressed fifteen years earlier during the traumatic event.

She had been holding on to so many pent-up emotions and feelings. Eventually, she had to allow the pain to rise to the surface, turn toward it, and allow these painful feelings in. After working through her emotions and feelings with many tears, an emotional memorial service had a healing effect. She could eventually allow closure.

"Don't let yesterday take up too much of today" - Will Rogers

How attuned are you to your emotions and or feelings?

Answer the following questions to assess how attuned you are to your feelings and or feelings. Explore and improve your emotional awareness, which can be so helpful in managing your anxiety and overall well-being.

Emotional Awareness:

How often do you take time out to see how you are feeling?

____

____

Can you identify your main emotions when you experience them?

____

____

Identifying your Emotions:

Do you find it challenging to name a specific emotion you may be feeling?

____

____

Do you understand the specific triggers or causes of your emotions?

____

____

Physical Sensations:

How aware are you of the physical sensations connected with your emotions (e.g., shallow breathing, the tension in the body, a racing heart?)

____

____

Can you identify how your body responds to different emotions?

____

____

Feelings in your Relationships:

Do you find it easy to pick up on the emotional needs of people close to you?

____

____

Are you in touch with the emotional aspects of your relationships and if they're challenging or positive?

____

____

How you deal with your emotions:

Are there specific emotions that you find more challenging to navigate?

____

____

How do you manage intense emotions? Are they healthy or potentially harmful?

____

____

Expressing your emotions:

Do you feel comfortable sharing your feelings with others, or do you often keep them to yourself?

____

____

How does expressing or not expressing your emotions impact your relationships?

____

____

Dealing with Anxiety:

How does being aware or unaware of your emotions connect to your anxiety?

____

____

What specific emotional triggers linked to your anxiety can you identify?

____

____

FEELINGS EXAMPLES AND LIST YOUR OWN FEELINGS

Complete the Emotional Awareness Table to identify and record your feelings related to anxiety. It encourages self-awareness and helps you tune into your emotions related to your anxiety:

Emotional Awareness Table:

Example of Feelings connected to anxiety	✓	**Write Your Own Feelings**
Fearful		
Nervous		
Scared		
Worried		
Terrified		
Panicked		
Ashamed		
Overwhelmed		
Distracted		
Tense		

"Anxiety is a thunderstorm. Be the umbrella of mindfulness that protects you from its turmoil" – Kate Hudson-Hall

Mindfulness as a solution

QUESTION: How would you like just to press that pause button on your anxiety-infused mind and give yourself a break?

ANSWER: Well, this is how mindfulness can help you... So, what are you waiting for? Let's dive right in, grab that pause button, and learn what other advantages await you.

What is Mindfulness?

Mindfulness is learning to pay attention purposefully and nonjudgmentally in the present moment. **It's as simple as that!**

Are "you" ever in the present moment?

Most people are not! We're either:

Worrying about the past: what could have been, or what you thought happened compared with what actually happened. Yes, some of us are fantastic at using our imagination to embellish the most impressive stories!

Worrying about the future: what could happen, or worrying about worrying! We are like a worrywart on steroids, whatever a worrywart is! And what comes with worry? That darn anxiety.

Sometimes, it's okay

Of course, it's okay to spend some time thinking about the past, daydreaming or planning the future, and pinpointing any looming issues connected to past experiences that may have happened for self-preservation or self-protection.

But if thoughts and feelings connected to past events or something that may or may not happen in the future constantly distract us, spending time in the present moment is something that hardly ever happens.

Oh yes, then it all becomes a refined habit, constantly mulling over something said seven years ago, igniting our anxiety, and then the build-up that will happen again engulfs us.

What is the present moment?

Hearing a loud bang outside or seeing a beautiful view would bring us back to the present moment, and the here and now is where we want to be.

Practicing mindfulness will give you a break from the constant, never-ending chatter in your mind. You will think clearer, be less distracted, calmer, and more relaxed. Who wouldn't want more of this?!

How wonderful would it be to have an internal pause button on your anxiety-infused mind?

The research is mind-blowing.

Much research has been carried out on the multiple benefits of mindfulness, with studies on groups of people who have had MRI scans on their brains before taking an eight-week mindfulness course and then another MRI scan once they had completed the course. The findings are astonishing.

Are you ready to be astonished?

They found that particular brain areas had either shrunk or grown in response to the regular mindfulness

For example:

The amygdala—part of the brain known for its role in stress and anxiety—had reduced and became smaller.

The prefrontal cortex—part of the brain responsible for controlling emotions, concentration, and problem-solving—had become thicker.

Not only does the amygdala shrink after mindfulness practice, but the connection between this and the prefrontal cortex also becomes less responsive! Therefore, you will be less reactive, allowing other brain areas to strengthen and connect with attention and concentration.

Imagine having a sharp, shimmery memory.

Practicing mindfulness also affects an area of the brain called the hippocampus, which is responsible for your memory. MRI research found that this also became thicker after practicing mindfulness. . . and who doesn't want a better memory?!

Therefore, your brain is effectively being rewired, and your reaction to everyday stresses of life often reduces your anxiety. You will find you react with a sense of calmness, empathy, and understanding.

Studies show it can relieve several psychological and physical issues. For example:

- Anxiety
- Obsessive thoughts
- Stress
- Depression
- Low self-esteem
- Chronic pain
- Insomnia
- Lower blood pressure

Why do we want to be in the present moment?

Standing present in the moment is the only time we ever have to be alive, make decisions, grow, heal, and be there for the people we love.

Being present and practicing our ability to be mindful not only makes us happier but can also help us:

- Increase our skills to cope with negative feelings like anxiety, anger, and fear,
- Deal with pain more successfully, and
- Reduce our stress.

Informal and Formal Mindfulness

Learning how to stay in the present moment

There is informal and formal mindfulness. Let me explain the differences between the two:

Informal Mindfulness is consciously weaving mindfulness moments into your everyday routines by engaging in the present moment with gentle awareness.

Formal Mindfulness is planning an intentional, regular commitment of time to practice mindfulness. This kind of practice is called mindfulness meditation.

HOW TO PRACTICE INFORMAL MINDFULNESS

YOU COULD FOCUS ON A CROCUS

So, rather than focusing on your thoughts, give yourself something else to focus on. For example, focus on breathing, preparing food, brushing your teeth, showering, washing up, or on your feet.

If focusing on your feet, pay attention to all the sensations you can become aware of with your feet. Ask yourself, is there:

- Tension
- Tingling
- Pressure
- Aching
- Warmth, or coolness

Keep focusing on your feet. If your mind wanders off. . . on purpose, without being judgmental, bring your mind back to your feet and into the present moment.

Each foot contains 26 bones. (This means more than one-quarter of the bones in your entire body are found in your feet!) Whether you are focusing on your left or right foot, each has 33 joints, 19 muscles, 10 tendons, 107 ligaments and probably a lump of cheddar cheese! So, plenty for you to focus on.

By focusing on your feet, you will be paying attention on purpose and nonjudgmentally in the present moment. It's as simple as that to give yourself the break you so deserve. In the beginning, it may not be so easy. You may last for three breaths. Then your mind does major shopping in your head.

With compassion and kindness, gently return to your feet or breath and refocus. The more you do this, the less your mind will bother you, showing you that you have the power of choice rather than being dragged into a cab.

Each time your mind wanders off, this is a magical sign you are practicing mindfulness the correct way; be proud of yourself. You are strengthening your mindfulness skills.

Regularly and with patience

Do ten minutes a day to start. When you start to see the benefits, do fifteen minutes and build from there.

"You can't stop the waves, but you can learn to surf" - Jon Kabat-Zinn

TECHNIQUE: HOW TO PRACTICE FORMAL MINDFULNESS

Here we go, the steps to your mindfulness practice…. Mindfulness Breathing

Commit for ten minutes by setting the alarm on your phone. Find somewhere quiet-ish. Then, find an upright, comfortable chair, but not too comfortable. We don't want you snoring! Place your feet flat on the floor, hands palms down on your legs. If possible, close your eyes.

1. Focus and relax into your body. Feel the connection with the chair and your feet on the floor. This brings you to the present moment.

2. Start by being aware of your breathing. Take one deep breath and then breathe normally. Where do you feel this, in your chest or tummy? Focus on this area.

If your mind drifts off to an anxious thought, acknowledge it and allow it to be there. As best you can, imagine it as a cloud floating by. (If your mind wanders too much and you are not finding this easy, maybe do this for five minutes to start!)

3. What feelings are here? Turn toward any sense of unpleasant feelings and acknowledge them without trying to make them different from what you feel.

4. What body sensations are here right now? Imagine a scanner scanning your body to pick up any tightness or tension sensations and acknowledge them, but again, do not try to change them.

5. Again, bring your focus back to your breathing. Use each breath as a chance to anchor yourself into the present moment. Of course, again, if your mind wanders off, kindly and nonjudgmentally bring it back to the area of your breath you are focusing on.

When you are ready, allow yourself to come all the way back into the room.

Excellent, you did it. Mindfulness helps you stay with your anxious feelings without pushing them away or trying to suppress them. Allowing yourself to feel and acknowledge your anxiety and other feelings often helps them dissipate. They become less powerful and loosen their hold over you.

There are multiple ways to practice mindfulness. In the Mindfulness Practice Options Table, explore these methods. With a checkbox for tracking your progress and additional benefits, discover which ones work for you and incorporate them into your daily routines.

Mindfulness Practice Options Table:

Mindfulness Practice	Checkbox ✓	Benefits
Awareness of Breath: Focus on your breathing, paying attention to each in-breath and out-breath		Reduces stress, increases focus, enhances self-awareness
Body Scan: Gradually scan your body, noting all different sensations, including tension in the shoulders		Promotes relaxation, eases physical tension, heightens body awareness
Mindful Eating: Eat slowly, savor each bite, and notice the flavors and textures		It helps develop a healthy relationship with food, enhances the enjoyment of meals
Nature Observation: Spend time in nature, observing the sights, sounds, and sensations		Increases connection to the environment boosts mood
Guided Visualization: Imagine a calming scene or experience in vivid detail		Reduces anxiety, enhances creativity, cultivates positive emotions
Mindful Walking: Walk slowly, focusing on each step and the sensations in your feet and body		Combines physical activity and mindfulness, clears the mind
Gratitude Practice: Reflect on things you're grateful for, big or small		Changes your focus to positive aspects of life, increases overall well-being
Loving-Kindness Meditation: Cultivate feelings of love and compassion by repeating positive phrases for yourself and others		Cultivates compassion, enhances self-esteem, creates positive relationships
Mindful Coloring or Drawing: Engage in coloring or drawing, paying attention to each stroke, pattern, color and your creativeness		Enhances and deepens present-moment awareness
Journaling: Write about your thoughts, feelings, and experiences without judgment		Encourages self-reflection, provides emotional release, tracks progress over time

THE "EMOTION SURFING TECHNIQUE"

Another powerful way to help you calm yourself is with the "Emotion Surfing Technique." Again, rather than trying to distract yourself from your unbearable anxiety, sit with that complex emotion or feeling and use your breath and attention to ride the wave out. Turn toward it rather than fight it. Go with the sensations you're thinking and feeling and ride them like a professional surfer rides the waves.

Letting yourself feel and recognize your anxiety can guide your tense feelings to disperse gradually. As they lose their power over you, this weakens their grip.

Your anxiety is similar to a wave that sweeps over you. It starts as a ripple in a calm seabed. Then, as it slowly drifts forward, it builds up, becoming bigger and bigger until it finally crashes onto the seashore and then calmly recedes. It continually returns in this never-ending cycle.

We might not have control over the enormous anxious feelings or fifteen-foot wave right now, but we can learn to surf and go with it.

It's time to tune in to and identify, observe, and process your mind-body connection as you reap the rewards of feeling calmer and happier.

Mindfulness guides you toward creating space around your anxiety, so it doesn't saturate or consume you.

Are you ready to overcome that anxiety? Are you ready to learn to surf without water?

TECHNIQUE: The "Emotion Surfing Technique"

Here we go. Let's practice another mindfulness tool.

1. Find a quiet, comfortable place where you won't be disturbed. Close your eyes and focus your attention on your breathing.

   Feel the air coming through your nostrils into your chest, lifting and falling, your stomach rising and falling. Focus on all aspects of your breathing, and if you notice your mind wandering off and thinking about something else, kindly, not judgmentally, bring it back to your breath.

   Do this for approximately two minutes. To help you focus on your breathing, think to yourself as you inhale, "breathe in," and exhale, "breathe out."

(If your anxiety becomes too much, bring your focus to another part of your body for example your feet. Stay with the awareness of your feet until you feel ready to focus again on your anxiety.)

2. When you're ready, in your mind's eye, tune into your anxiety or imagine a difficult situation that causes you anxiety, then sit back and notice:

   Where in the body do you feel the unbearable anxiety? (For some, it may be their stomach or chest.)

3. Once you're aware of where you feel the unbearable anxiety in the body, become aware of the sensations
   connected to your anxiety, and just observe them.

Notice how the anxiety is like waves. See if you can tune into it as it builds up, eventually hits a peak and subsides. Imagine you're a professional surfer, and use your breath to help you ride the wave.

Stay with the sensations as they begin to build again, notice the peak, and then be aware as it dissolves back down.

The anxious feeling may change. It may be a little swell, then change to a massive tidal wave, but stay with whatever comes up.

As the wave begins to build, imagine standing on a surfboard and riding the waves—surf, surf, surf.

Great, you're a real surfer; you've done it! Congratulations! You can be present, experience your anxiety, and not react. You now have begun to break free from your anxiety. Fabulous!

Whenever you feel the anxiety building, take time out and start surfing your anxiety. In the beginning, see how long you can stay with it. Set a timer. Start with five minutes, then build up to ten, fifteen, and so on.

Study and research show us that turning toward a difficult emotion nonjudgmentally, with compassion, improves your mental health and your physical health.

"YOU ARE OK. RIGHT HERE. IN THIS MOMENT."

Client example for the "Emotion Surfing Technique:"

Meet Sarah, a 25-year-old marketing professional navigating the high tides of anxiety in both her work and personal life. Sarah often found herself overwhelmed by the pressure of deadlines and the fear of not meeting expectations. Traditional strategies to distract herself from anxiety don't seem to work. So, I taught her the "Emotion Surfing Technique."

Before the technique:

Sarah felt overwhelmed, anxiety crashing over her. Knots in her stomach and tightness in her chest were routine, especially before stressful meetings or challenging tasks.

Introduction to the technique:

I introduced the "Emotion Surfing Technique" as a way to ride emotional waves rather than resist them.

The Teaching of the "Emotion Surfing Technique:"

Sarah started with mindful breathing. The rhythmic inhales and exhales became her anchor. I encouraged her to let thoughts come and go without judging them, gently bringing her attention back to the breath each time her mind wandered off. This initial mindfulness exercise laid the groundwork for the upcoming surfing.

Riding the Anxiety Waves:

When Sarah felt ready, he mentally tuned into a situation that typically triggered anxiety. She identified the physical sensations in her body, mainly centered around her stomach. I then guided her to observe these sensations as if they were waves – building up, reaching a peak and then subsiding.

Surfing the Anxiety:

With each breath, Sarah imagines herself on a surfboard, skillfully riding the waves of anxiety. I prompted her to stay with the sensation, recognizing the peaks and valleys. Sometimes, it felt like a gentle swell and other times, it resembled a massive tidal way. The key is for her to say with it, just like a surfer navigating the unpredictable ocean.

Progress:

As Sarah practiced, she noticed subtle shifts. The anxiety, which once was an overwhelming force, started to lose its grip. Initially setting a five-minute timer, Sarah gradually extended her surfing sessions to ten, then fifteen minutes. The more she surfed her anxiety, the more she realized that she could withstand the waves – they didn't define her.

So, through the "Emotions Surfing Technique," Sarah found a unique approach to anxiety. Learning to ride the waves allowed her to be present with her emotions. She was skillfully navigating life's currents.

"Every experience, no matter how bad it seems, holds within it a blessing of some kind. The goal is to find it" - Buddha

Track your mindfulness journey and observe how it influences your thoughts and feelings. Using the example table, fill in the details as you practice and reflect on your experiences.

Mindfulness Example Table:

Date	Mindfulness Practice	How I Felt Before	How I Felt After
	Body Scan Mediation	Tense and stressed	Grounded and relaxed
	Mindful Breathing	Overwhelmed with anxiety	Calm and centred
	Mindful Eating	Busy	Present and satisfied
	Mindful Journaling	My mind was a muddle	Clarity and calmer
	Mindful walking in nature	Overcome with emotions	Connected and tranquil

Mindfulness Tracker Table:

Date	Mindfulness Practice	How I Felt Before	How I Felt After

Remember, mindfulness is a skill that takes practice. As you engage in different mindfulness exercises, consider how they affect your emotions and overall well-being. Over time, you may find mindfulness an invaluable tool for managing your anxiety.

EXTRA TOOLS FOR YOUR TOOLBOX TO A CALMER YOU

In this Hackster, you've learned about the complexities of feelings and emotions and how understanding and managing them can significantly impact your everyday life.

Let's refresh your way to success with the key takeaways you have learned:

Understanding Feelings and Emotions:

- Emotions are automatic physical reactions if we are happy or fearful.
- Feelings are reactions to your emotions. These happen when your brain assigns meaning to your emotional experience, which can become even more specific than an emotional response.

The consequences of suppressing feelings:

- Ignoring or suppressing feelings can lead to anxiety, depression, eating disorders, anger, addiction, low self-esteem, and so much more.
- As you begin to open up about your feelings, this will prevent emotional issues and physical consequences and promote your emotional well-being.

Mindfulness as a solution:

- Mindfulness is the awareness that arises by learning to pay attention on purpose and non-judgmentally in the present moment.
- There are two ways to practice mindfulness: informally by focusing on your breath or formally by meditating.
- The huge benefits include reduced anxiety, feeling calmer and positive physical brain changes.

Remember that mindfulness is a skill that requires practice. By taking time to experiment with the different mindfulness exercises, you can effectively manage your anxiety and improve your mental health.

How to Practice Mindfulness:

- There are two different ways to practice mindfulness:

  Informal Mindfulness involves weaving mindfulness moments into daily routines by focusing on specific tasks.

  Formal Mindfulness is setting aside time for meditation and structured mindfulness exercises.
- Practicing both informal and formal mindfulness methods will allow you to reduce your anxiety, increase self-awareness and help to cope with daily stress and negative emotions more effectively.

Mindfulness Practice Options:

- **Informal Mindfulness:**
  Awareness of Breath. Focusing on your breathing will help reduce stress and build self-awareness.

- **Formal Mindfulness:**
  The Body scan. Scanning your body will help to ease physical tension and heighten body awareness. It is excellent for beginners as you draw awareness over your whole body.
  Or Emotion Surfing. Learning to ride the waves of your thoughts and feelings to relax and calm your busy mind.

As you explore different mindfulness practices, you can:

- Choose the ones that work best for you, incorporate them into your daily routines, and create positive habits along the way.
- Observe how mindfulness influences your thoughts and feelings, gradually reducing your anxiety.

"You are stronger than you think. Remember to stand tall" - Chantal Lavaute

Review and Reflection:

Now, it is time to take all you have learned and begin to question yourself. Discover your behaviors and patterns and how you can begin to change them.

1. **Understanding Feelings and Emotions:**

What feelings and emotions do you find most challenging?

Identify the feelings and emotions that you struggle with the most. Are there specific events or triggers that bring up these feelings?

What can you learn about your emotions and feelings and how they impact you?

---

2. **The consequences of suppressing feelings:**

How do suppressed feelings contribute to your anxiety and other issues?

___

___

What are practical ways to begin to open up to your emotions and feelings? (For example, acknowledging your emotions and allowing yourself to feel without judgment.)

___

___

Can you think of an experience where acknowledging your feelings led to a more positive and healthier outcome?

___

___

Maybe now is the time to understand that suppressing or ignoring your feelings can harm your daily life, such as increased anxiety, stress or even physical. To work with this, maybe open up to a trusted friend, family member, or therapist about what is going on for you and how you feel. Journaling is a great way to express your feelings safely. As you begin to change this habit and express your emotions and feelings more positively, you might find your anxiety reduced. Maybe look into the possibility of professional therapy if you have been carrying these feelings for a long time.

Then, create a feelings journal to unravel the patterns of your behaviors and why they occur.

3. **Mindfulness:**

   Why is mindfulness a valuable tool for managing anxiety, and how does it help you stay present in the moment?

___

___

How can you begin your mindfulness practice, and what are the essential steps to incorporate mindfulness into your daily life to reduce your anxiety?

Write down how you will go about this.

---

4. **How to practice mindfulness and mindfulness practice options:**

How can mindful eating, nature observation or loving-kindness meditation contribute to reducing anxiety, and what are their specific benefits?

What are some informal techniques to practice mindfulness throughout the day, and how can these moments of mindfulness benefit your overall well-being?

Hop back to the table and find which mindfulness techniques you want to practice. How can you introduce mindfulness into your daily life to help manage your feelings? For example, set reminders on your phone daily to stop and practice mindfulness for 3 minutes. Go through the different ways to practice mindfulness, find what works for you and begin your list. Gradually increase the amount of time practicing as you become more comfortable.

What is formal mindfulness?

What are the steps involved in practicing it effectively to manage anxiety?

Think about what steps you could take to create time in your everyday life to practice mindfulness, and then create a tailored mindfulness routine that would work with your lifestyle, making it a sustainable and accessible tool for reducing your anxiety. For example, create 5-10 minutes in the morning or evening and use the body scan technique, which is excellent for beginners, to help them become more in tune with physical sensations and feelings.

Step one:

Step two:

Step three:

Hackster 4: And Finally:

As we conclude the enlightening journey of Hackster 4, brace yourself for the upcoming adventure in Hackster 5, where we delve into the intricacies of worrywart thoughts. From understanding when worrying thoughts become problematic to challenging negative thoughts, I'll equip you with tools to combat negativity. Plus, we'll demystify EFT – what it is and how it works. Your path to a calmer, more empowered mindset continues in the next huckster. Let the transformation unfold.

"Anxiety happens when you think you have to figure out everything all at once. Breathe. You're strong. You got this. Take it day by day" - Karen Salmansohn

HACKSTER 5

DO YOU WANT SOME MAGIC TO REDUCE YOUR ANXIETY?

**"Anxiety is a storm that can't last forever.
After the rain, there's a rainbow of strength waiting" – Kate Hudson-Hall**

What You'll Learn in Hackster 5:

This Hackster is dedicated to helping you understand and manage those nagging worrywart thoughts and anxiety that can often plague your mind. In this journey, we'll explore how to identify these thoughts, the reasons why anxiety reinforces itself and the powerful techniques to regain control and find calm amidst the storm of anxious thinking. The Emotional Freedom Technique(EFT). Consider it your pocket-sized magic wand, ready to diminish anxiety and propel you toward an inspired and motivated mindset. Let's dive right in!

Here's a sneak peek of what else lies ahead:

How to Identify Your Worrywart Thoughts:

- Oh yes, you will be learning how to empower yourself to distinguish between your everyday concerns and the worrywart thoughts that can significantly contribute to anxiety.

The "Spin and Win Technique:"

- This powerful technique involves tuning into your emotions and imagining them as something physical with your body. By working with the "Spin and Win Technique! You'll learn how to reprogram the way these emotions affect you and reduce your anxiety rapidly.

EFT Tapping: Also known as the "Emotional Freedom Technique:"

- EFT tapping introduces a life-changing method of managing negative thoughts and feelings by tapping specific points on your body. You'll discover how to effectively harness this magic wand to address anxiety.

Remember your thoughts are not unchangeable truths, and you possess the strength to choose how you react to anxiety. In this hackster, you'll learn techniques to spin your world from chaos into calmness or help you tap your way to a more peaceful life. So, let's get spinning while we tap.

Serene Breaths Unleashed: Dive into tranquility with Hackster 5's signature technique!

Revitalizing Humming Bee Breath (Bhramari):

The humming bee breath, or Bhramari Pranayama, is a calming and centering yoga breathing practice that can be super beneficial for relieving anxiety and stress and improving sleep.

It's time to experience instant calm and conquer stress and anxiety with the unique sensation of the humming bee breath.

Prepare for serenity: find a cozy seated position on the floor or a chair with feet flat on the ground.

Relax and close your Eyes: gently close your eyes and let the tension melt away.

Inhale, Press, and Hum:

Inhale deeply through your nose. As you exhale, press your fingers into the tragus cartilage, that tiny flap in front of your ear canal. (This blocks out external sounds.)

Keep your Mouth Closed and Make a Loud Humming Sound:

With your mouth closed, begin to make a steady, low-pitched humming sound. Feel the vibrations in your head and around your face. Focus on the sensation and sound.

Continue for as long as Comfortable:

Maintain the humming sound for as long as it feels comfortable. You can experiment with the pitch and intensity of the humming to find what works best for you.

Conclude Mindfully:

After you've practiced for a sufficient duration, release your fingers from the ears and take a few moments to sit quietly. Notice how you feel and observe any changes in your state of mind.

The effects of Short-term Practice of Bharamari Pranayama on sleep quality and perceived stress in school students:

A study published in 2021, available in the International Journal of Physiology https://ijop.net/index.php/ijop/article/view/2603 evaluated the effects of Bhramari Pranayama practice on sleep quality and perceived stress in school students.

The results were astounding. **After just a few weeks of Bhramari Pranayama practice, there was a significant improvement in sleep quality and reduced perceived stress.** As you have learned, there is an excellent link between stress and anxiety. So, let's get breathing!

Ancient Indian texts on Yoga describe, "As the breath moves, so does the mind, and mind ceases to move as the breath is stopped"

HOW TO IDENTIFY YOUR WORRYWART THOUGHTS

Are you a worrywart?

Can you differentiate between ordinary worrying thoughts and those that might cause concern?

Worrying is normal

We all worry about certain up-and-coming events that maybe we are unsure about. It is that apprehensive feeling or overly concerned worry about a situation or problem. It is normal, and usually, the worrying thoughts disappear.

Normal worrying thoughts:

- **It's the norm:** It's perfectly normal to have flapping worries about daily issues, such as an up-and-coming social event or work meeting. These worries don't hang around long and don't significantly impact your everyday life.
- **Motivate you:** Worrying thoughts can fire you into action. For example, worrying about an upcoming presentation might prompt you to spend more time preparing for it.
- **Helps to resolve problems:** Natural worrying often resolves when you find solutions to change an issue, and then once you have addressed the problem, the worry often dissolves.

When worrying thoughts are a problem:

- **Overload of worrying thoughts:** If you are worrying about everything and anything when there is no immediate threat, this could signal you have generalized anxiety disorder (GAD). Which disrupts your everyday life.
- **Physical symptoms:** If you are excessively worrying, this could lead to physical symptoms such as headaches, sleep disturbances, tension and digestive issues, which could signal an anxiety disorder.
- **Uncontrollable, invasive thoughts:** If your worrying thoughts become uncontrollable, invasive and repetitive, this may indicate obsessive-compulsive disorder (OCD). It affects your everyday life, which can be highly distressing.

Have you ever noticed that many of the thoughts zapping through your mind tend to be more on the negative side? Research suggests that approximately a whopping 75% of our daily thoughts are negative.

Here are the reasons why:

- Brain protector: Our brains are naturally wired to pay close attention to negative happenings. It's like a survival mechanism that has been around since our ancestors. To keep us safe, the focus is on potential dangers, like that saber tooth tiger hunting for prey. So, your brain tends to focus on the negative.
- Becomes a habit: if you keep thinking negatively, it becomes habitual and a neverending habit loop of gloom.

- Social Media Stress: Social media can send your brain into a nose dive of doom and gloom. Ever find yourself comparing yourself and feeling down as you scroll through social media where everyone seems to be having that perfect life, and you don't?
- Anxiety and Stress: When you're engulfed in stress or a bundle of anxiety, it's like a switch in your brain to churn out any slithery negative thoughts it can find.
- Blame the Media: So much of the news on tv tends to focus on bad news. This may make you think the world is scarier than it is.

But do you believe what you tell yourself to be true?

Your worrywart mind tells you that you need to worry, analyze and look into every nook and cranny (whatever a cranny is! It sounds rather rude!) to find reassurance about everything and anything. It calls you names, tells you that you are going mad, stupid, and everything else it can to belittle you. It is one big fat beast of a bully.

Even though it says such wicked things about you, the problem is you believe it. You take heed. (Whatever also is a heed?) You trust every word you tell yourself—giving that bully respect.

LISTEN UP NOW. THIS IS IMPORTANT… YOUR THOUGHTS ARE NOT FACTS

- **NOT true,**
- **NOT important,**
- **JUST A THOUGHT,**
- **AND THOUGHTS ARE NOT FACTS.**

So, if you continue to listen to everything it tells you, it will not be easy to begin breaking your anxiety pattern. It's time to learn how to change the record.

Let's get flippin' that vinyl!

Find your key (and no, I don't mean your door key!)

Yes, trying to avoid anxious thoughts or situations may help you feel better and feel good, but because it feels good, it reinforces your anxiety. It's a vicious cycle.

The key is identifying the triggers that cause your anxious cycle to begin, which you have done in Hackster 3. You'll be able to stop it sooner if you learn to recognize it before it becomes uncontrollable. Being skillful at anything requires time and effort, so be patient.

Turn toward your worrying thoughts and face them head-on. To reframe your fearful thoughts, ask yourself questions like:

"What would be the worst thing that could happen?"

"What is the worst-case scenario?"

You can see a more rational view of the problem by evaluating the facts back and forth.

QUESTIONS: REFRAME YOUR THOUGHTS:

Complete the questions using the examples and start to combat your negative thoughts.

What am I worried about:

Is this worry based on assumptions or facts?

Have I faced similar experiences before, and how did they turn out?

What is the worst-case scenario?

Am I dramatizing or exaggerating the outcomes?

"What would be the worst thing that could happen?"

Is there a more positive way to look at this situation?

What's the best course of action I can take right now to work through this concern?

Flip the Script

Now, it's time for a flip and a shift. Take a step towards altering those negative thoughts, turning them into more neutral or positive ones. Review your list of thoughts and explore how you can reframe each situation.

Think of a specific situation you want to begin breaking the pattern of. Then, complete the Thought Record Table.

Thought Record Table:

Date	Situation	Current Feelings	Current Thoughts	Alternative Thoughts	Alternative Behaviors
Example:	**Walking home from work in the dark**	**Anxious Scared Lonely**	**Someone is going to attack me I am feeling overwhelmed**	**I'm at some risk, but not as bad as I tell myself. The street is well-lit, and I've walked it many times without any issues**	**Take deep breaths, in for 4, hold for 8 and out for 8**

Congratulations on completing your 'Thought Record Table! You've taken a significant step in understanding and challenging your negative thoughts. Ready to embark on the journey of transformation? Let's hop on forward.

"Our anxiety does not empty tomorrow of its sorrows, but only empties today of its strengths" - Charles Spurgeon

Are you ready to learn this genuinely incredible technique to calm your anxiety in less than five minutes?

Let's get down to it with **The "Spin and Win Technique."**

So, suppose you feel anxious about being anxious or just can't stop worrying about everything and anything. If this is you, I will teach you a fantastic technique to help you reduce any negative feelings you may have linked to your worrywart mind in less than five minutes, so listen up.

Before we begin, let me explain the magic of this technique. All emotions can be felt in your physical body. For example, when you feel happy, scared or excited, you recognize that emotion because you can actually feel it in your body.

So when you tune in and can feel that emotion in your body, you can use that incredible imagination to move it and change it in many different ways using the submodalities you have learned about in Hackster 1.

So when you use the "Spin and Win Technique," you will take an emotion or feeling and imagine it as something physical within your body.

For this exercise, you're going to focus on the feelings of being anxious, such as:

- Fearing something could go wrong,
- Feeling stressed,
- Feeling upset or
- Looking stupid in a social setting.

We will work with these to change how you feel with this technique, so stay focused. Wahoo, here we go; this is brilliant, and it works!

TECHNIQUE: "THE SPIN AND WIN TECHNIQUE"

Let's begin:

1. Think of a situation that triggers the anxious, nervous, restless, or tense feeling. Using your anxiety scale, rate how intense your anxiety is. Where does that anxious feeling start? Where in your body would be the first time you're aware of that anxious feeling? People often say in their stomachs, but that's where it ends up, so I really want you to tune in and ask yourself where this anxious feeling starts.
Is it in your forehead? Or your throat or in your chest, and then moves to the knot in your stomach? This would be the path of the feeling.
2. For that anxious feeling to remain there, it would have to spin forward, backward, or to the right or left because those are the only two possibilities geometrically.
If you aren't sure or think it isn't moving at all, I want you to tune into that anxious feeling by pointing to it and asking yourself which way it's spiraling.
3. Now, take either index finger and move it in a circle clockwise or counterclockwise. Whichever way the anxious feeling is moving, get in tune with it. Imagine a circle with arrows. Give the circle color, make it red and spin it, moving whichever way the fearful, anxious feeling moves.
4. Now, reverse the direction of the spin; make the circle purple and spin it in the opposite direction. Next, spin it faster, now faster still, and notice what happens. The anxious feeling will start to spin backward faster and lessen.
5. Return to your scale and see how the feeling has reduced.
Keep spinning and taking yourself back through these steps to reduce your anxiety.

So, whenever you are aware of that nervous, anxious feeling, get spinning as often as possible.

To watch extra videos where I show each technique,
join the Bonus Companion Course at: https://anxietyhacks.info/info-step1/

A "Spin and Win Technique" client example:

Meet Elizabeth, a 38-year-old juggling the wild ride of parenting three energetic kids. Stress is like a daily companion to her. In the session, I taught her the "Spin and Win Technique."

Identifying the Starting Point: Elizabeth rated the intensity of her anxiety triggered by her kids screaming at her. She identified the starting point of this feeling, which often manifested in her chest.

Understanding the Movement: I then guided Elizabeth to recognize the direction of the anxious feeling – whether it spun forward, backward, to the right or left.

Initiating the Spin: Elizabeth used her index finger to mimic the imagined circle in the direction of the anxiety's movement. Elizabeth gave the circle the fiery red color and spun it accordingly. She visualized the anxious feeling moving with the spin.

Reversing the Spin: Elizabeth reversed the spin by changing the circle's color to a pastel violet. She noticed the anxious feeling lessening as she imagined the spin speeding up.

Reassessing Anxiety Intensity: Returning to her anxiety scale, Elizabeth gauged how much the feeling had reduced. I encouraged her to repeat the process, spinning faster each time.

Progress

Elizabeth incorporated the "Spin and Win Technique" whenever she sensed the familiar knot of anxiety. Practicing this consistently, she found that the anxious feelings were losing their grip on her. The technique became her go-to tool to swiftly reduce her stress and anxiety.

On her next appointment, Elizabeth told me, "The Spin and Win technique is nothing short of amazing! It's like having a superpower over my anxiety. Before, those anxious thoughts would linger, but now I can literally spin them away. It feels so liberating to have this tool. I've used it so much when the kids are fighting with each other or just driving me crazy, and the difference is incredible. It's not just about reducing anxiety. It's about feeling in control. This tool is a game changer for me."

The "SPIN AND WIN TECHNIQUE" LOG TABLE

Track your transformation and see just how powerful this technique is. Believe me, it is a show-stopper!

The issue to spin on	Rate on the scale before	Rate on the scale after

"Nothing diminishes anxiety faster than action" - Walter Anderson

TECHNIQUE: THE "EMOTIONAL FREEDOM TECHNIQUE" (EFT)

Grab your fingertips, and let's get them to work the magic—
your leap to freedom from your anxiety with EFT!

So, one fantastic tool to help you is another terrific technique to help reduce your anxiety and any negative thoughts and worries you're having right now, sometimes in less than 90 seconds! I will teach you a specific technique called Emotional Freedom Technique (EFT for short or the tapping technique.)

EFT therapy is like a best friend to keep in your pocket to help you anytime you are feeling anxious or have any negative feelings.

So many of my clients have hugely benefited from tapping whenever they have negative feelings. They're amazed by how quickly this process can reduce these anxiety-ridden devils, or some may call feelings they may be having.

The good news is by learning EFT:

- It's a quick therapy; you won't need to relive painful memories.
- Once you've learned the points, you can tap on any problematic feelings.
- You can take it wherever you go if you're uneasy. You can do a round of tapping to reduce the uncomfortable feeling.

Let me tell you now that it's very bizarre. But it's mighty in reducing any undesirable feelings you may be having. It's described as acupuncture but without the needles. It involves tapping on acupressure points on the body while thinking about any negative behavior, feeling, or habit you want to stop or change.

It's a very safe and gentle tapping procedure, using just your fingertips to tap directly on points on your face and body.

How does EFT work?

EFT works with your body's energy, which flows through your body along pathways called meridians. Disruptions in our energy create negative feelings and behavior patterns. Once you find those energy disruptions, you use the tapping process to correct them with focused wording as you tap on nine specific points on the face and body.

Your focused wording helps you tune in to the painful thought or feeling, pointing you to the energy disruptions you will change and reduce.

As you tune in to your specific issue, the tapping stimulates the energy pathways and balances your energy disruptions. It only takes minutes to dissolve negative feelings.

HERE'S HOW YOU ARE GOING TO CHANGE NOW WITH EFT:

Using the fingertips of your index and middle finger of either hand, you tap approximately 5-7 times on each point.

Firmly but gently tap either side of the body as outlined below:

- **KC: The Karate Chop point (abbreviated KC). This is found at the center of the fleshy part of the outside of your hand (either hand), between the top of the wrist and the base of the baby finger. Or the part of your hand you would use to deliver a karate chop.**
- **EB: At the beginning of the eyebrow just above and to one side of the nose.**
- **SE: On the bone bordering the outside corner of the eye, on the side of the eye.**
- **UE: On the bone under an eye about 1 inch below your pupil. Under the Eye.**
- **UN: On the small area between the bottom of your nose and the top of your upper lip. Under the Nose.**
- **CH: Midway between the point of your chin and the bottom of your lower lip. Even though it's not directly on the chin point, we call it the chin point because it's descriptive enough for people to understand easily.**
- **CB: The junction where the sternum (breastbone), collarbone, and the first rib meet.**
- **UA: On the side of the body, at a point even with the nipple (for men) or in the middle of the bra strap (for women). It's about 4 inches below the armpit.**
- **TOH: On the top of the head. If you draw a line from one ear, over the head, to the other ear, and another line from your nose to the back of your neck, the TOH point is where those two lines would intersect.**

To watch extra videos where I show each technique, join the Bonus Companion Course at: https://anxietyhacks.info/info-step1/

THE 5 STEPS OF THE EFT TAPPING BASIC RECIPE

1. Identify the specific feeling that you're going to tap on. (Only focus on one particular negativity at a time.) Examples might be feeling scared, hopeless, worthless, panicky or, although you could tap on any negative feeling you're having.

2. Test the initial intensity: please think of your anxiety scale between 0 and 10, with 0 being the feeling that has gone entirely and 10 being its most intense. This gives you a guide, as you'll review your scale after each round of tapping to compare the progress.

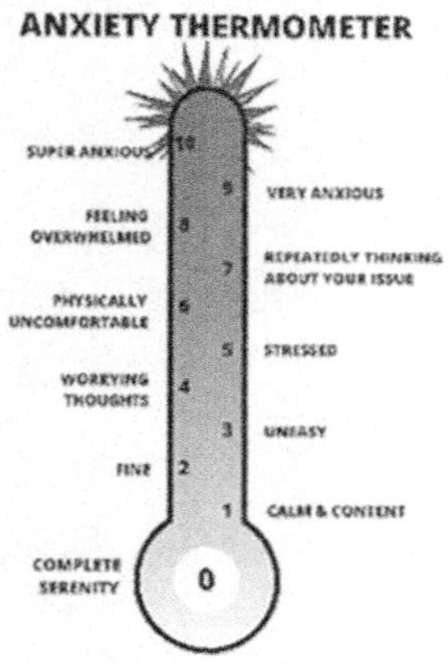

If you're tapping on a feeling, you can recreate the memories in your imagination to make it easier to gauge where you would be on the scale.

If you're tapping on physical pain, tune into the pain and assess the level.

3. The next step is to repeat a simple phrase while tapping continuously on your karate chop point (KC). You would do this by saying:

"Even though I have this_______________, I deeply and completely accept myself."

Fill in the blank for whatever specific emotion you're working on.

For example:

- Even though I'm so stressed because of work, I deeply and completely accept myself.
- Even though I feel overwhelmed with anxiety, I deeply and completely accept myself.
- Even though I'm anxious about developing a serious disease or other health issues, I deeply and completely accept myself.
- Even though I can't stop worrying about …., I deeply and completely accept myself.
- Even though I feel I have no control over my anxiety, I deeply and completely accept myself.
- Even though I'm anxious about losing my job or about money worries, I deeply and completely accept myself.
- Even though I'm anxious about attending parties or social events, I deeply and completely accept myself.
- Even though I feel overcome with fear and anxiety about making this speech, I deeply and completely accept myself.

To see a video demonstration of EFT, join the FREE Bonus Companion Course link: **https://anxietyhacks.info/info-step1/**

EFT to reduce stress

One study from 2020 implies that EFT may reduce by 43 percent the stress hormone cortisol levels. Also, it suggests an improved immune system and reduced blood pressure.

National Library of Medicine: https://pubmed.ncbi.nlm.nih.gov/32162958/

Example of The Emotional Freedom Techniques Tapping Points:

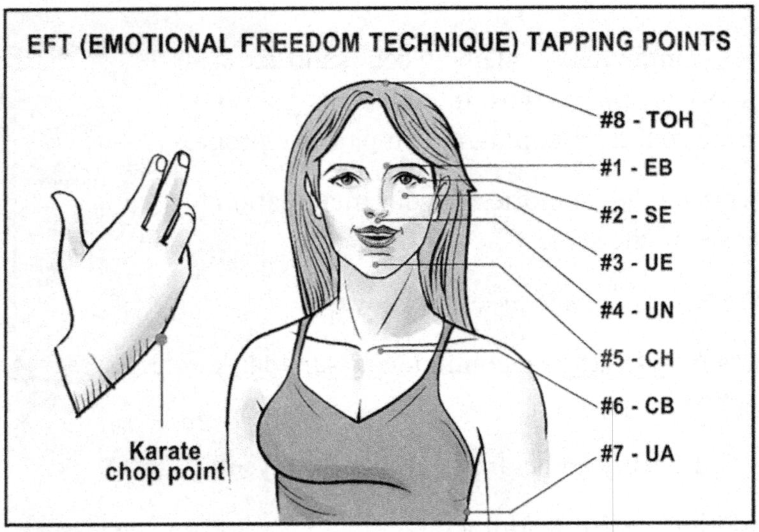

When you think about your anxiety, what thoughts and feelings come up?

Now that you've learned the EFT process, you will put this into practice. It's an incredible way to reduce your anxious thoughts and feelings.

So, when you think about addressing your anxiety, what worries you? What's stopping you from moving forward?

Using the EFT Table Log Tracker, complete a list of your anxious thoughts and feelings connected to your anxiety and where you would be on your scale. Then, spend time tapping on that specific thought or feeling; the goal is to reduce this to a 0.

EFT Table Log Tracker:

ANXIOUS THOUGHTS AND FEELINGS CONNECTED TO YOUR ANXIETY	SCALE BEFORE	SCALE AFTER
Example: "Even though I am scared I will lose control, I deeply accept myself."	9	0

It's essential to address all the different thoughts and feelings that come with the word "anxiety."

Where are your anxious feelings now?

With EFT, you can start to push open that squeaky old door, let in a little light, and have a peek. You may be surprised at the warmth and happiness the light brings you.

Where are your anxious feelings now? Are they still lurking? If they are, it's time to tap, tap, tap.

As you become more aware of what's genuinely causing your anxiety, continue tapping on whatever negative thoughts or feelings may arise. Enjoy the huge benefits as the worrying and anxious feelings begin to reduce, opening you to more positive feelings. This will help guide and motivate you to continue working through other thoughts and feelings that come up.

Each day, I want you to spend at least fifteen minutes (more would be so much more beneficial!) tapping through your list of negative behaviors and then moving on to feelings, emotions, and thoughts.

Okay, there you have it. This incredible magic tool is right in your fingers, so keep tap, tap, tapping on all your destructive thoughts and feelings.

EXTRA TOOLS FOR YOUR TOOLBOX TO A CALMER YOU

Within this Hackster, you have learned the importance of identifying your anxiety habits and how avoiding situations or trying to control everything can increase your anxiety.

The key takeaways you have learned are:

How to identify your worrywart thoughts:

- You have learned to distinguish between your normal and problematic worrying thoughts.
- Understood the importance of realizing that your thoughts are not facts and CAN be changed.

The "Spin and Win Technique"

- By tuning into an emotion or feeling and imagining it as something physical in your body, working with the "Spin and Win Technique," you can reprogram how the feeling affects you.
- You discovered how to use the "Spin and Win Technique" to reduce your anxiety rapidly.

EFT Tapping: Emotional Freedom Technique

- You have learned that tapping on specific points on the body can reduce negative thoughts and feelings, which is an incredible tool to manage anxiety.
- Work with specific experiences of anxiety, like money worries, social events, losing control or health concerns, by tapping and working through negative feelings.

Remember that your thoughts are not facts, and you have the strength to choose how you react to anxiety. So, if you're not spinning, you'll be tapping your way into a calm life.

"You have within you, right now, everything you need to deal with whatever the world can throw at you" - Brian Tracy

Review and Reflection:

Answer these questions to help you understand what you have learned in this Hackster and how you can use it to create a calmer you:

How to identify your worrywart thoughts:

If you are a worrywart, what worry patterns have you developed, and how have they impacted your behaviors?

If you have noticed worry patterns where you often magnify small-scale issues, taking a molehill and creating a mountain out of it, and the pattern has led to anxiety, stress and physical symptoms like stomach ache or headache.

What could you do differently? (For example: Practice mindfulness and begin to challenge irrational thoughts when they come forward.)

In what ways does avoiding a situation contribute to the escalation of your anxiety? How can turning towards your anxious thoughts, instead of avoiding them, help in managing your anxiety?

What strategies can you use to expose yourself gradually to your anxiety triggers, and why is this exposure considered beneficial in reducing anxiety levels?

The "Spin and Win Technique"

- Why is it crucial to understand the path of your anxious feelings and the direction in which they move when applying the "Spin and Win Technique"?

- List three examples of when you could use the "Spin and Win technique" to manage your anxiety.

EFT Tapping: The "Emotional Freedom Technique"

- How does EFT work to dissolve negative feelings and modify thought patterns?

- How can you effectively create a personalized EFT routine for addressing your anxious thoughts and feelings? List three ways you will address your anxious thoughts and feelings with EFT and include them in your routine.

  (Work with specific experiences of anxiety, like money worries, social events, losing control or health concerns by tapping and working through negative feelings.)

Hackster 5: And Finally:

As we conclude the empowering journey of Hackster 5, you've mastered the transformative "Emotional Freedom Technique" (EFT) and the "Spin and Win Technique." Now, buckle up for Hackster 6, where we'll dissect the intricate dance between your anxiety, those pesky habits and the dramatic "what if" scenarios. So, prepare for mental gymnastics on your path to lasting tranquillity. Let's roll into the next chapter.

Remember, if you always do what you have always done,
you will always get what you have always got.

HACKSTER 6

ANXIETY PATTERNS: IT'S GETTING TO BE ABIT OF A HABIT

"Anxiety is a puzzle. Don't search for missing pieces; create your own masterpiece of tranquillity" – Kate Hudson-Hall

What You'll Learn in Hackster 6:

In Hackster 6, we will explore the relationship between your anxiety, unhelpful habits and the often crippling "what if" thinking. Learning that anxiety can inadvertently lead to the formation of habits that aren't your fault but rather the result of your current mental programming right now. The great news is that with the power of affirmations, you can transform your mindset and refocus your life.

Here's a sneak peek of what else lies ahead:

Anxiety habits

Anxiety is a complex spider web of confusion, and often, it results in the creation of habits that aren't in your best interest. These habits are typically linked to past experiences and reinforced through repetition. We'll begin by building your awareness to help you recognize your patterns, triggers and typical responses.

Creating New Habits:

Your key is breaking free from unhelpful habits, starting with one specific, achievable, positive habit and replacing it. Breaking down this new habit into manageable steps to help you stay focused on your journey of change.

Habit loop:

You'll gain an understanding of the habit loop and its three essential components:

- The trigger (Which can be a thought, feeling or event)
- The routine (the habit itself) and
- The reward (the payoff or relief)

We'll explore how habits linked to your anxiety can range from behaviors like excessive alcohol consumption, binge eating or teeth clenching.

The "Shatter That Habit Technique":

This technique involves a powerful visualization process. How to visualize your current habit, the triggers, and the negative routine, and then rapidly shift to envision a new positive habit replacing the old one.

Crushing your "What If" Thinking:

We will be focusing on recognizing and breaking the cycle of "What if " thinking, which often leads to anxiety and worry. You'll learn about the benefits of challenging the belief that "What if" thinking protects you from disastrous outcomes and how it can shift toward a more positive outlook, which is essential in reducing anxiety.

Affirmations:

Affirmations are practical tools for reshaping your thinking into positive patterns. We'll delve into the art of crafting effective affirmations.

So, in this hackster, we will work together to break free from the shackles of unhelpful habits and "What if" thinking and instead build a foundation of positivity and empowerment.

Serene Breaths Unleashed: Dive into tranquility with Hackster 6's signature technique!

Relax with the MindfulEase Serene Breeze Method

MindfulEase Serene Breeze Method is also known as mindful breathing. You will harness the power of mindfulness, anchoring your attention in the present moment, which is where we all want to be.

Prepare for serenity: Find a comfortable seat, and begin with open or closed eyes.

Inhale through the Nose:

Inhale deeply through the nose, allowing the tummy to expand gently with each breath.

Exhale Gradually through the Mouth:

Release the breath slowly through the mouth, establishing a rhythmic pattern.

Focus on the breath Cycle:

Once settled, concentrate on the inhalation through the nose and exhalation through the mouth, syncing with the rise and fall of the tummy.

Observe Thoughts Without Judgment:

Acknowledge any thoughts that enter the mind without judgment. Let them pass gently, like clouds floating by, and redirect your focus back to the breath.

Continue Until Calmness Sweeps In:

Maintain this mindfulEase Serene Breeze Method until a sense of calmness prevails. Gradually draw your awareness to observe how the body and mind feel.

Increase your well-being and calmness with the MindfulEase Serene Breeze method, a wonderful blend of intentional breath and mindfulness. Follow these steps as and when you feel the anxiety, stress or tension building for a serene journey to calmness and self-awareness.

Taking mindful breathing pauses throughout the day can reset the nervous system, fostering continuous calmness.

ANXIETY HABITS AND WHAT YOU NEED TO KNOW

So what is a habit?

Habits are routines we automatically do, which act as shortcuts that allow us to use our energy in more critical areas of our lives.

We've created positive habits that can enhance our lives, but anxiety often leads to not-so-good habits.

Having anxiety isn't your fault!

It's the natural result of your mental programming at this moment in time, and it's become an unconscious automatic behavior. Understanding this is the first step to change.

Anxiety Habits: Learned Behaviors that Can Be Unlearned

Anxiety habits are repetitions of behaving, thinking and feeling that we have developed over time due to different stressors, situations or life experiences. Often, these habits work as coping mechanisms. But they can become damaging and lead to chronic anxiety.

The good news

Anxiety habits are learned behaviors that can be unlearned.

Past experiences: Anxiety habits are often linked to real experiences. For example, suppose you have had distressing or traumatic experiences in the past. In that case, your body and mind have learned to react with anxiety to situations that are similar to that encounter. This is a learned association between your anxiety and a trigger and is the route of many anxiety habits.

Strengthened over time: These anxiety habits are strengthened over time by repetition. When you encounter a trigger that makes you anxious, your habit is to respond with anxiety. Over time, this repetition strengthens the connection between the trigger and the anxious response.

Unlearning Anxiety Habits: You can unlearn your anxiety habits. The first step is awareness by recognizing your patterns, specific triggers, and how you typically respond to them, and then challenging your learned responses. It's a process of rewiring your brain to develop positive habits and responses.

First, let's look at YOU and what habits you have created. For example:

Avoiding situations

- Avoiding certain situations that make you feel anxious often increases the anxious feeling.
- The more you avoid a situation, the more you fear it, and the anxiety becomes overwhelming.

Uncertain about everything

- Do you battle with wanting to know every detail about an upcoming event?
- Do you try to be in control of everything? Of course, this isn't possible, as whatever you do will involve some uncertainty. It's that fear of unpredictability.

Consistently fighting your negative thoughts

- Trying to suppress negative thoughts often has an adverse effect.
- Those darn negative thoughts, the more you try to fight these off, the more you try not to think about them, the louder they shout. Acceptance can weaken their power.

Embracing your Feelings

Changing habits and patterns involves changing your outlook. Rather than battling with your anxious feelings, what about if you allowed them to be there?

This powerful habit change can lower anxiety's effect on you. Accepting that it is okay to feel what you feel—just allowing them to be there.

Questions to help you begin Unravelling Habits

Becoming more self-aware is a crucial step in identifying and understanding your habits related to anxiety. Complete the list of questions to help you become more aware of your anxiety habits:

When do I feel most anxious during the day?

____

____

What specific situations or triggers consistently make me anxious?

____

____

What are the physical signs that I'm feeling anxious? What is the first sign?

____

____

What thoughts go through my mind when I'm anxious?

____

____

Are there any patterns in my anxious thoughts?

____

____

How do I typically react when I'm anxious?

____

____

Do I have any negative behaviors to relieve my anxiety?

____

____

Are there any specific habits related to how I cope with stress?

____

____

Do I share my anxious feelings with others, or do I tend to keep them to myself? If I don't, how and to whom could I share with?

____

____

How you created your habits

It takes conscious action and practice to form your habit. Therefore, it takes intentional action and training to break your habit. Or better still, replace it with an excellent positive habit.

Let's begin to understand your habit cycle. You can't change a habit without understanding how they work individually for you. What precisely are the steps?

There are three steps to the process, it's called the Habit Loop

A trigger – A thought, feeling, image, something you see or hear. This could be that you hear someone talking about going to a party where he doesn't know anyone, which fires up your anxiety.

A routine – The habit. In kicks your worrywart mind. Your mind is worrying over a party you have been invited to and how you imagine all sorts of negative scenarios: you making a fool of yourself or talking in front of people who won't like you even though you haven't met them. The anxiety fires up, and you get a stomach ache.

A reward – A distraction. You reach out for a glass of wine or cookies.

Earlier in the book, you began to identify your anxiety's specific triggers and rewards. So, you engage in your habit or worry about everything to gain some reward like numbing your emotions, relieving boredom, or time for yourself.

Examples of rewards:

- Relief by overeating or drinking alcohol
- Weight loss
- Release of dopamine
- Comfort
- Detachment from feelings

Then, if there's repetition, the habit develops.

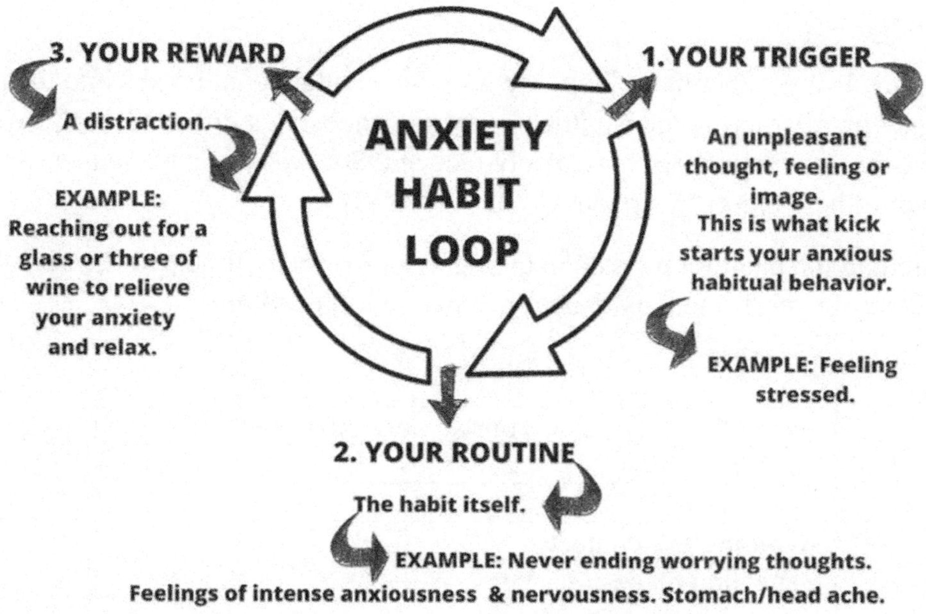

Client example: Meet Claire, a 33-year-old. Here is how I guided her through the maze of her anxiety habit loop. We first identified her triggers, dived into the routine and uncovered the sneaky rewards that were fueling her anxiety dance.

Understanding Triggers:

Claire often found herself drowning in anxiety when thinking about her responsibilities at work, especially when deadlines loomed = her anxiety trigger.

Unpacking the Routine:

The routine was a well-choreographed worry dance. Her mind went into overdrive, imagining all the ways things could go south at work. The routine had become so ingrained that it was second nature.

Revealing the rewards:

Claire's routine earned her a temporary escape. That worry dance, as uncomfortable as it was, provided a brief distraction from stress. In the grand scheme, it was her mind's way of finding relief.

The Habit Loop Unveiled:

After I had explained the habit loop to Claire, it was like turning on a light in a dark room. She could see the cycle clearly – trigger, routine and reward. It was like decoding her anxiety pattern, and that awareness was the first step towards change.

Embracing a Shift:

We discussed the power of embracing her feelings. She started acknowledging it instead of trying to shut down the worry dance. Telling herself, "Okay, here's that anxiety again." It was about changing the music to find a more empowering beat.

Claire's Transformation:

As Claire became more aware of her habit loop, she introduced intentional breaks into the routine. She'd pause when the trigger hit, disrupting the habitual worry and choosing a different response. It wasn't an instant fix, but over time, the intensity of her anxiety reduced. She was just a passenger in her habit loop: she became the conductor of her anxiety symphony.

For Claire, understanding the habit loop was like giving her a roadmap. It helped her navigate her mind, offering a sense of control over the anxiety dance she once felt trapped in.

Habits that connect to your anxiety might be:
Teeth clenching
Leg shaking
Avoiding eye contact
Canceling plans
Becoming bored easily
Jaw grinding
Nail-biting
Procrastinating
Binge eating
Plus, so many more

Identifying Your Anxiety Habits

Let's take a closer look at the habits you might have developed that are connected to your anxiety:

Avoiding Situations

Avoiding situations you find anxiety-inducing often makes the anxious feeling worse.

The more you avoid, the more you fear the situation, and anxiety grows.

Uncertainty and Control

Do you struggle with the need to know every detail of an upcoming situation?

An overwhelming need to be in control can lead to anxiety because life inherently involves uncertainty.

Fighting Negative Thoughts

Attempting to suppress or fight negative thoughts often backfires.

The more you resist them, the stronger they become. Acceptance can diminish their power.

The want to feel "normal."

Many people with anxiety desire to feel "normal," like those who remain calm and undisturbed by their feelings.

Setting high expectations and demanding that you should feel a certain way exacerbates anxiety.

Embracing Your Feelings

Change involves a shift in perspective. Rather than fighting your anxious feelings, try allowing them. This simple yet powerful habit change can reduce the impact of anxiety on your life. Accept that it's okay to feel however you feel.

Now you have more of an idea of your habits, let's break this down even further:

To create a clear picture of your habits, completing a habit diary is a great way to understand the patterns connected to your habits. Make your habit diary based on this habit diary.

When completing your habit diary, write everything down when you're aware of the habit rather than at the end of the day, as you can forget what you thought and felt when the habit occurred.

Remember, this isn't about changing the habit at this point but becoming aware of the links and triggers that cause the pattern.

The Habit Diary Log:

DATE/ TIME	YOUR TRIGGER THOUGHTS, FEELINGS AND IMAGES JUST BEFORE THE HABIT	YOUR HABIT	THOUGHTS, FEELINGS AND IMAGES DURING THE HABIT?	THOUGHTS, FEELINGS AND IMAGES AFTER THE HABIT?	YOUR REWARD/ PLEASURE?	NEW REPLACEMENT HABIT
Example	**Getting dressed, jeans feel tighter. "I'm fatter." Image of bulges over tops of jeans. Feel anxious & angry**	**Overeating to calm anxiety**	**"I can't stop. I am hopeless." Image of eating more. Feel helpless, sad & frustrated**	**"I am worthless." Image of me alone forever. Feel anxious, lonely, a failure**	**Starving yourself all day and then binge-eating**	**List 3 ways to calm yourself when anxious. 1. The CALM your Alarm Technique 2. Start Journaling 3. "The Spin & Win Technique"**
1.						
2.						
3.						
4.						
5.						
6.						
7.						
8.						
9.						
10.						

Once you have completed your diary and become conscious of your triggers, habits and rewards, it's time to replace old habits with new ones, and repetition is the key.

Now, the fun part. . . Creating a new habit.

The more you repeat your new habit, the more your brain will cement the new neural pathways. Therefore, the more you stop the old habit, the more you'll stop the old habit. How incredible is that! Wahoo, so off we go…

Great, it's time to decide on the new positive habit you will create.

Start by deciding on one positive habit you would like to create. Start with a small habit, allowing you to be better prepared and see your focus more clearly. Empowering you to feel more motivated will be more manageable and achievable.

The key is to be specific. Break down the big picture of the new habit you will create.

But hang on. . . let's look at what not to do first.

Many of my clients are not specific about what their new habit will be.

Here's an example of habits that are too general: "I want to stop stressing about everything."

"I want to stop overthinking."

These probably aren't going to become actual habits, as they are too vague. It's time to break that picture down into smaller chunks. For example:

"When I get home from work, the first thing I'm going to do is to practice mindfulness or listen to a relaxation recording to calm myself and relieve my stresses of the day."

Or, "I will begin practicing the Emotion Surfing Technique once a day."

These are better because they're more accurate.

In your habit diary, complete the last column with your new habit or a specific replacement habit connected to your old habit.

Keep replacing old habits with new, powerful, positive habits as you become aware of them.

But what happens to your brain when you begin to create a new habit?

Creating a new positive habit can be powerful and lead to beneficial and encouraging life changes. We're all creatures of habit. We rely on our past, learned behaviors, and habits to make decisions.

Here's the exciting part: it's all down to neuroplasticity, meaning your brain's ability to change. Consequently, we can adapt and reorganize how our brains are wired.

When creating a new powerful habit, you're also creating new positive neural pathways in your brain. Thus, that old habit— the old neural pathway in your brain—becomes weaker. It wears off in time, making room for new neuro pathways to form. That's why creating a healthy, new, positive habit is easier than continuing the old one.

How long does it take to create a new habit?

In the past, psychologists believed it took twenty-one days to create a new habit. New research shows that developing helpful new positive habits takes sixty-six days. Of course, everyone is wired differently; it could be less for you!

It's time to commit to making the change.

Creating the old habit may have taken time, so this isn't an overnight fix. It will take some time. So, make that commitment because if you aren't going to do it, no one else can! You can do this. But you have to decide to give this your full attention and commit to making this change.

Your steps to changing your habits.

Repetition is the key to creating this new habit. Staying inspired to focus on your new habit may not be easy initially. But it's essential to take one day at a time.

Imagine how you might be in two months from now, having achieved your goal of changing this habit.

Tell friends and family of your intentions to help reinforce and encourage you to stay focused.

After you have completed your habit diary and created powerful positive habits to replace that old decaying beast of a pattern, here's how to break your unwanted habit:

THE TECHNIQUE: THE "SHATTER THAT HABIT TECHNIQUE"

This is an excellent technique to help you stay motivated and permanently change your old habits.

You'll be stepping out of the old you and then seeing yourself how you would like to be in the future, making that image so powerful that it attracts you to become drawn into the kind of person who is free from that old unhelpful habit.

Here we go with the powerful habit changer:

Step	Instructions
1.	Now that you've identified your habit, I want you to visualize yourself doing that habit, including what happens just before this habit begins. Step into this image, looking through your own eyes. Set that picture aside. This is your trigger picture.
2.	Now, create your new positive habit. Make an image of this. Make it large, bright, and colorful of yourself already having this new habit. In this image, you can really see your sparkle. Your posture has changed, and you look happy and relaxed. What would you be saying to yourself? How would you look? How would you feel? Now, reduce that image, shrinking it to a small dot.
3.	Now, bring forward the old and the new habit. Then, when you're ready, imagine yourself participating in the old habit.
4.	Now, imagine pulling your positive image, as if it's on strong elastic, back as far as it will go, then have the new habit picture rapidly explode and fly into the image of you doing the harmful habit. See that old habit smash into minuscule pieces as you say the word "swishhhhh" with the new positive habit image replacing the old habit image.
5.	Now blank the screen as if the TV has lost its connection.
6.	Repeat the process faster this time. As you do this, the new positive habit image comes alive with you happy, positively practicing your new habit as the negative image loses color and fades away into the far distance.

Swish, swish, swish. Keep repeating the whole process at least five more times, getting faster each time.

Then repeat the whole process twice daily, morning and night, until the excellent habit becomes embedded and you're no longer unconsciously doing the bad habit.

To watch extra videos where I show each technique, join the Bonus Companion Course at: https://anxietyhacks.info/info-

By understanding your anxiety habits, you can work towards transforming them into more positive, constructive behaviors. The journey to overcoming anxiety begins with these crucial insights and a commitment to change.

"The greatest weapon against stress is our ability to choose one thought over another" - William James

"What if" Thinking

Are you on the carousel of "What if " chaos?

Are you trapped in the relentless cycle of "What if" questions?

One by one, do you create a huge, overwhelming tower of worry?

Let's get real – this pattern isn't useful or helpful. It is your anxious mind playing tricks on you.

If this is you, then it is time to learn how you can crush this "what if " pattern and drawback control of your thoughts:

Step outside: The first step is being aware that you're caught in a whirlwind anxiety cycle of "What if"s. Recognize that your mind is circling with these unhelpful questions, intensifying your anxiety.

Challenging the "What if" trap: Understand that your "what if " thinking is tricking you into thinking you are in control. You can protect yourself from disastrous outcomes by believing you are thinking this way about every possible scenario. This trickster needs to be challenged.

Statistics prove that 95 percent of your "what ifs" never actually happen! So, what a waste of time and energy!

Crushing the "what if" pattern

What if I told you that you can begin to change this annoying "what if" habit into your friend for change?

Best and worst cases: Instead of slipping down into that "what if" well, channel your inner curiosity and ask yourself

- **"What is the worst-case scenario here?"**
- **"What is the best-case scenario?"**
- **"I will deal with that if and when it happens."**
- **"I will cross that bridge when I come to it."**

Yes, when you first start to look at a more optimistic scenario, it may not feel completely comfortable. It's like changing any old dusty habit. It takes conscious effort and determination and is a powerful way forward.

By challenging your "what ifs," you are creating two fantastic changes:

- **Giving your mind a pause for thought, a break from that never-ending wicked inner critic.**
- **It is breaking the pattern of endless, unhappy automatic thoughts.**

Client example: Meet Simon, a 29-year-old navigating the rollercoaster of "What if" chaos. His mind seemed to have a mind of its own, conjuring up endless scenarios that left him on edge. Here's how we worked through it:

Step Outside the Carousel:

Simon first became aware of this carousel of "What ifs" during our sessions. He noticed the anxious questions piling up and recognized that it wasn't helping him.

Challenge the What If Trap:

Understanding that this pattern was a bit of a trickster, Simon started questioning its validity. He realized that thinking about every possible disaster wasn't really keeping him in control.

In Reality:

We delved into the statistics. Simon discovered that, in reality, most of those "What ifs" never actually happened. It was like his mind was playing a game that statistics proved wrong.

Crushing the "What if" Pattern:

Now, the game-changer turns "What if" into an ally. Instead of spiraling down, Simon decided to play a different game. We discussed the best and worst-case scenarios. "What is the worst that could happen, and what is the best?"Simon told himself he'd deal with situations if and when they occurred.

Results:

As Simon began challenging his "What ifs," he felt a shift. It wasn't an overnight transformation, but with each scenario he tackled differently, he noticed a pause in those endless anxious thoughts. It was like the carousel slowed down.

Simon learned that curiosity about the best-case scenario was a powerful way forward. It wasn't about avoiding problems but facing them more optimistically. The "What if" chaos lost its grip, and Jake felt more in control of his thoughts.

So, he was no longer trapped in the relentless cycle but riding the waves of uncertainty with a newfound sense of empowerment.

Here are some ideas to help you begin to address those worrying "What if" thoughts:

"What if" Example Table:

What If Scenario	Best-Case Scenario	Worst-Case Scenario	Practical Steps to Change
What if I fail my exams?	I'm really good at exams!	I'll retake them	Create a study diary and ask for help if you need it
What if I run out of money?	I'll start to be more cautious of my finances	I'll have financial problems	Start to save, create a budget plan and search for a side income
What if I'm not good enough?	I'll be great and prove myself	I won't be so confident	Learn new skills, build on your confidence and believe in yourself
What if I make a mistake?	I can only learn from my mistake	I'll be reprimanded	Apologize if needed, correct the mistake and move on
What if I never change?	I'll grow and develop	I stay in the same place	Create positive goals and new habits for self-development
What if I can't find love?	I will meet an incredible partner	I'll stay single	Set yourself goals, start to socialize more, be open and start a new hobby
What if I have to speak in public?	I present a perfect presentation. They love me	I make small mistakes and get nervous, like everyone else	Create a plan of what and how to say. Prepare cue cards. Focus on the audience, not your gibbering chitter chatter
What if I open up about my feelings?	The relationship will improve	They may not understand and respond positively	When you are ready, find the right time, and be honest with yourself and them
What if all my plans fall apart?	New doors will open	I'll feel sad	Stay flexible and refocus
What if I never change?	I'll grow and develop	I stay in the same place	Create positive goals and new habits for self-develpment

"What if" Worries Log Tracker

Complete the table to help you address your "what if" thinking patterns and start to rewire your brain to

"What if" Worries Log Tracker:

What If Scenario	Best-Case Scenario	Worst-Case Scenario	Practical Steps to Change
What if they don't like me	Of course, they'll love me	They might think I am stupid	Be yourself, and focus on making new connections

"The only limit to our realization of tomorrow will be our doubts of today" - Franklin D. Roosevelt

AFFIRMATIONS

What is an affirmation?

An affirmation is a short, simple, positive phrase you repeat to yourself throughout the day to redirect your thinking and speaking into positive thought patterns. So, to help and soothe your racing mind, creating an empowering affirmation will help refocus your mind and bring it to a calmer, more positive place.

Your affirmation should be a phrase that instantly creates a compelling picture of yourself, looking and feeling the way you want to be, calm and at ease.

Again, this is working with our unconscious mind to guide it toward helping you move forward in your life, clearly telling it you're taking responsibility for change.

It's having a conscious, specific phrase to help create something new or help reduce something from your life.

Here are some hacks for creating and using effective affirmations:

- **Be positive and use the present tense.** Create your affirmations in the present tense as if they are already happening.
- **Be believable:** Create a phrase that you genuinely believe. This should feel achievable. If they're too far-fetched, they may not be effective.
- **Be worded in the positive and not contain negative words:** Use positive words and do not include words such as "not," "don't," "can't," or "mustn't;" otherwise, the unconscious mind won't hear the word "don't" and will focus on the next word.
- **Use I Statements:** Personalise the affirmation and make it more impactful by using "I" or "my" pronouns.
- **Hook into your Emotions:** Connect with the emotion behind your affirmation. Feel the positivity, excitement or calmness connected with it.
- **Repeat Regularly:** Consistency is the foundation. Practice this daily, repeating the affirmation as many times as possible, eventually building up to over one hundred times a day. Oh yes, my clients raise an eyebrow when I tell them this. But by breaking this down into blocks of twenty, it's incredible how quickly you can repeat your powerful positive affirmation.

Check out the affirmation examples. Which ones resonate with you?

Affirmation Examples Table:

Situation & Thought	Negative Thought	Positive Affirmation
General Anxiety	"My anxiety controls me"	" I am in control of my anxiety"
Feeling Stressed	"I'm too stressed. I can't handle this"	" I can manage stress, and I am resilient"
Social Anxiety	"Everyone is judging me"	"I can do this. I am confident"
Before a Presentation	"I am going to embarrass myself"	" I am well prepared and can handle this"
Feeling Overwhelmed	"I can't handle this"	" I can take one small step at a time"
Coping with Change	"Change is scary"	"I can cope with whatever the outcome is"
Overcoming Fear	"I'm too afraid to try"	"I have the strength and courage to overcome my fears"
Self-Doubt	"I'm not good enough"	"I am resourceful and worthy"
Relationship worries	"They'll eventually leave me"	" I am worthy of love and secure in my relationships"
Overwhelmed with Anxiety	"I'm always anxious about something"	"I am calm and in control of my thoughts"

Now it's your turn. Create your own realistic and suitable affirmations using the Affirmation Creation Table.

The Affirmation Creation Table:

Situation & Thought	Negative Thought	Positive Affirmation
Stress and Anxiety Overload	"I feel I am ready to snap"	"It's okay to say NO for the sake of my mental health"

EXTRA TOOLS FOR YOUR TOOLBOX TO A CALMER YOU

In this Hackster, you've learned how anxiety can lead to unhelpful habits and how "What if" thinking can exacerbate your anxiety, but with affirmations, you can refocus.

The key takeaways you have learned are:

Anxiety Habits

- Anxiety often leads to creating not-so-good habits, which aren't your fault but the result of your current mental programming.
- Anxiety habits are learned behaviors, often linked to past experiences and reinforced through repletion.
- Unlearning habits begins with awareness of recognizing your patterns, triggers and typical responses.

Creating New Habits:

- Starting with one specific achievable positive habit and repetition is the key to creating a new habit and weakening the old one.
- You learned how important it is to break down your new habit into manageable steps to help you stay focused.

Habit Loop:

- You understand now that the habit cycle involves three steps: a trigger (a thought, feeling or event), a routine (the habit itself) and a reward (the payoff or relief).
- Habits linked to your anxiety can range from binge eating, drinking too much alcohol or teeth clenching.

The "Shatter That Habit Technique":

- You have learned that the "Shatter That Habit Technique" involves a powerful visualization process where you visualize your current habit, the triggers and negative routine, then rapidly shits to envision a new, positive habit replacing the old one.
- The mind is rewired to accept the new positive habit by mentally shattering the old habit into minuscule pieces, effectively breaking the negative habit loop. Then, repetition is essential to make this technique as successful as possible.

Crushing your "What if" thoughts:

- Recognizing you're caught in a "What if " pattern is the first step to change, which creates a cycle of anxiety and worry
- You have learned the benefits of challenging the belief that "What if" thinking protects you from disastrous outcomes and can create a shift toward a more positive outlook, which is essential in reducing anxiety.

Affirmations:

- Learning how affirmations need to be short positive phrases that are used to redirect your thinking into positive thought patterns.
- Effective affirmations should be in the present tense, believable and free of negative words.
- Using "I" statements to connect with your emotions is incredibly beneficial when creating affirmations.

"Courage doesn't mean you don't get afraid. Courage means you don't let fear stop you" - **Bethany Hamilton**

Review and reflection:

Answer these questions to help you understand what you have learned in this

Hackster and how you can use it to create a calmer you:

Anxiety Habits
Now you understand habits and their importance. You can begin to evaluate your daily patterns to identify any potentially unhelpful habits connected to your anxiety. Using your habit diary, write down your thoughts, feelings and behaviors connected to your anxiety habit. Commit to writing these down each day to gain a better understanding of your triggers.
Once you have identified several negative habits, start practicing the "Shatter That Habit" technique to replace the old habit to regain control. Commit to creating a new habit and develop a daily schedule to practice and stay accountable.

Having identified your anxiety habits, create a list of triggers and the behaviors connected with them.

____

____

When you feel a trigger, pause and become aware of the routine and connected reward, making it easier to address the habit steps. Write down your habit's components/steps:

____

____

Creating New Habits:

What strategies can you create to make specific and achievable changes in your life and form new positive habits? List three new habits.

How do you plan to ensure the daily repetition of your new habits to cement them into your daily routines and gradually replace old, unhelpful ones?

Habit Loop:

How does understanding the habit loop help you in breaking down and addressing the habits that are linked to your anxiety?

What connections can you make between your own anxiety-related habits and past distressing or traumatic experiences, and how does this learning inspire change?

The "Shatter that habit technique":

After practicing with the "Shatter That Habit Technique," how has your awareness of your ability to break free from old, unhelpful habits changed?

___

___

What have you learned about your ability to visualize and create change within yourself through this technique?

___

___

Crushing your "What if" thoughts:

Start listening to what you tell yourself, and if you are a "what if" whiffer, then actively address these with best and worst-case scenarios. This will help to change from a negative mindset to a more balanced one, therefore reducing your anxiety. If you are a "what if" worrier, write three examples of when and where you think this way.

___

___

Challenge your "what if" worries and write down what is the best and worst-case scenarios.

Best case:

___

___

Worst case:

___

___

Affirmations:

Create daily affirmations that remind you of your power over your reactions and post them in the car and around your home. For example: "I choose to breathe in calmness and breathe out tension." Or " I have the strength to control my anxiety."

Which of the affirmation examples works for you?

How can you use these affirmations to help you cope with specific anxiety situations or feelings?

What first affirmation will you create and use, and how will you incorporate it into your daily routine?

Hackster 6: And Finally:

In Hackster 6, we bid adieu to your unhelpful habits, which, let's face it, were as useful as a chocolate teapot. Now brace yourself for the grand premiere of Hackster 7, where we consolidate your newfound wisdom. Connect the dots and craft a comprehensive strategy for managing your anxiety effectively. Get ready for the next phase of your transformative journey.

"You have the power to heal your life, and you need to know that. We think so often that we are helpless, but we're not. We always have the power of our minds. Claim and consciously use your power" -

Louise Hay

HACKSTER 7
JOINING THE DOTS....

"Anxiety is a ripple. Be the pebble of relaxation that creates still waters in your mind" – Kate Hudson-Hall

What you'll learn in Hackster 7:

In Hackster 7, you will be learning how to navigate the tumultuous seas of fear and anxiety and, by doing this, open the doors to serenity.

In this Hackster, we will weave together the knowledge and techniques you've gained throughout this workbook. It is time to connect the dots and create a comprehensive strategy for managing your anxiety effectively.

Here's a sneak peek of what else lies ahead:

The "C.A.L.M. Your Alarm Technique:"

- You will learn the mind-blowing "C.A.L.M. Your Alarm Technique," an acronym that will guide you through specific techniques: Concentrate, Action, Listen and Motivation. These powerful tools will assist you in reducing your anxiety, lowering stress levels, and boosting self-confidence.

Goal Setting:

- Setting goals is a crucial part of your journey. We'll teach you to take your big goal and break it down into smaller, manageable steps. Clear, specific goals provide motivation, purpose and clarity.

Technique Time:

- I will teach you how to create a list of the techniques you've learned throughout this workbook. You'll then create your practice plan by selecting the techniques that you find most beneficial for managing your anxiety effectively or boosting your motivation.

Your Personalised Anxiety Action Plan

- Overcoming anxiety requires a deep understanding of your behavior patterns and their connection to anxiety. You'll learn to create a Personalised Anxiety Action Plan, which includes a list of changes you need to make and what you will begin to do differently.

The Motivation Booster Technique:

- Motivation is the driving force that keeps you moving forward in your battle against anxiety. I will introduce you to the "Motivation Booster Technique," a powerful tool to help you maintain motivation during challenging times.

Let's take that final step in this journey and remember you're not alone.

Serene Breaths Unleashed: Dive into tranquility with Hackster 7's signature technique!

Discover Serenity: The RollRhythm Breath Exercise

The RollRhythm breath exercise is a dynamic technique that empowers you to engage your lung capacity fully. Start in a comfy position, and as you get used to it, you can adjust to whatever feels right for you.

Caution:

Warning: Initial attempts at roll breathing might make you feel lightheaded or dizzy. If there's a hit of hyperventilation, ease into it by slowing your breath and rising gradually.

Prepare for serenity:

Find a quiet, comfortable space to sit or lie down.

Position one hand on your stomach and the other on your chest.

Inhale and Exhale:

Inhale through your nose and exhale through your mouth for a count of eight to ten breaths.

Lung Filling Technique:

Concentrate on expanding your lungs, allowing your stomach to rise while keeping your chest steady.

Sequential Chest Breaths:

After eight to ten breaths, breathe in, first into your lower chest, then your upper chest. The hand on your stomach should fall a little.

Exhale with a Whoosh:

As you exhale, create a gentle whooshing sound with your mouth. Lower your hands from your stomach and chest down to your sides.

Duration:

Repeat this sequence for three to five minutes.

Breathing exercises are a portable tool for calmness, accessible anytime and anywhere with conscious effort.

The "C.A.L.M. Your Alarm Technique"

Anxiety management is more than just struggling your way through. It's about taking control of your life; the "C.A.L.M. Your Alarm Technique" is your lifeline.

What is the "C.A.L.M. Your Alarm Technique?"

The "C.A.L.M. Your Alarm Technique" is an effective tool created to help you reclaim control of your anxiety. It's a structured technique, an acronym, which guides you through a clear pathway to combat your anxiety.

You will incorporate four techniques into one swoop of a humdinging technique. With each letter of C.A.L.M., you will be guided to focus on one of four specific techniques you have learned.

What are the benefits of the "C.A.L.M. Your Alarm Technique?"

Reduce Anxiety Levels: By including this incredible technique in your life, you will become aware of a noticeable reduction in your anxiety levels.

Reduce Stress Levels: Regularly using this technique will empower you to gain more control over your emotions and provide you with the skills to better deal with your stress. Allowing you to respond to stressors with calmness and strength.

Sleep will improve: Managing anxiety with this technique will help to improve your sleep patterns. Many people who have used this technique report falling asleep quicker and sleeping more soundly.

Self-Confidence Increases: People who have used this technique to manage their anxiety naturally build self-confidence. Learning to trust their ability to handle challenging situations and approach life with more positivity.

Are you ready to learn the most dynamic instant tool you will ever need to calm your anxiety? Here we go, let's swoop on in.

TECHNIQUE: THE "C.A.L.M. YOUR ALARM TECHNIQUE"

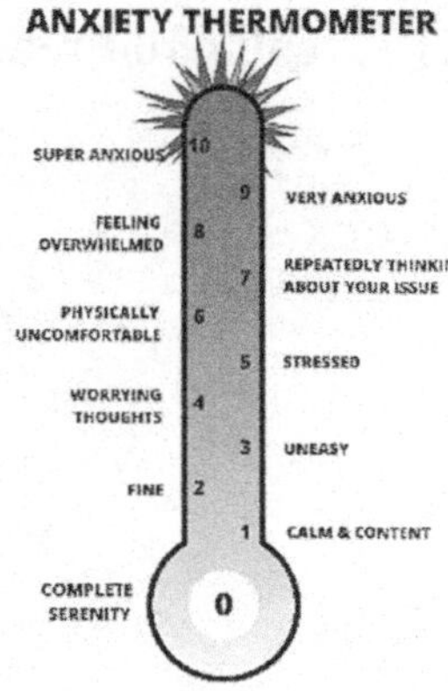

As you may have noticed, I like a good scale, but not when I eat a fish!

Before you start: Rate where you are on your anxiety thermometer scale with this technique.

As soon as you realize your anxiety has been sparked, tune into your anxiety and rate where you are on the anxiety thermometer scale.

HACK 1:

C is for "Concentrate." Concentrate on taking one deep, grounding, calming breath. (Or more if necessary)

Let me remind you (from Hackster 2) how to breathe, in case you have forgotten! Remember to make this the most beneficial deep breath possible to access your calm, parasympathetic nervous system.

C is for concentration. Take a deep, short breath in through the nose to the count of four (If you're Pinocchio, this may be longer! But try to keep it to a quick, short drag in) all the way down into the pit of your stomach.

Hold your breath for the count of eight. (Only if you can. If you feel like you might collapse at such length, then please do countless. I don't want you keeling over, smothered in calmness!)

Then, breathe out through your mouth to the count of eight. When you breathe out, purse your lips (why on earth is it "purse"? I have no idea; you are hardly holding money in your mouth simultaneously!) and gently blow like you're blowing out a candle or bubble.

Breathing this way causes changes in the brain that override anxiety and stress.

HACK 2:

A is for "Action." It is time to take action. Here we go with your "E.F.T." tapping talents.

You mastered E.F.T. in Hackster 5. It is a supersonic tool to have in your pocket for any negative feelings.

So, **A** is for action. Take action and begin tapping on your effective collarbone point on whatever negative thoughts or feelings may arise. Tap on either side or on both with both hands. Go at it like greased lightning for as long as you need.

Tapping on your collar bone point is specifically to calm and reduce your anxiety.

HACK 3:

L is for "Listening." Listen to your busy mind. What is it telling you right now to fire up your anxiety?

To eliminate toxic thoughts that contribute to your negative emotions, become aware of what you are telling yourself precisely.

L is for Listening. So next, use the thought-stopping technique from Hackster 5 and shout STOP at the negative voice, then tell it to "puff off" or get lost in whichever terminology works best for you—the stronger, the better, if you get my meaning.

Thought stopping diverts your attention from damaging repetitive thought habits.

HACK 4:

M is for motivation. Motivate yourself with your incredible imagination.

Using your imagination to get your motivating juices flowing can really help you down the road to positive change. In Hackster 6, you learned the power of visualizations.

M is for motivation, picture in your mind a positive image and a powerful anchoring phrase related to the situation, including how you want to feel. Make it so powerful that it will spin you into excitement about what you will do.

Depending on your situation, something similar to:

"I will be totally calm when giving this presentation." At the same time, visualize yourself speaking clearly and calmly to the group. **Say it, see it, do it!**

Once you have completed the four steps, take a moment to go back to your anxiety scale and rate where you are. If this isn't down to a 0, then zip back to the beginning and begin again. And again, if need be.

STOP! Stop what you are doing right now! Reread through the "C.A.L.M. Your Alarm Technique" and learn this powerful key to freedom.

Push the tissues aside, reach into your pocket, and grab this powerful technique when you are aware of your very first trigger that fires up like an explosive firework of anxious thoughts and feelings.

Learn it, feel it, and reap the rewards.

To watch extra videos where I show each technique, join the Bonus Companion Course at: https://anxietyhacks.info/info-step1/

YOUR BRIEF STEPS TO THE CALM YOUR ALARM TECHNIQUE:

STEP	TECHNIQUE DESCRIPTION	HOT TIP
Tune In	**Rate your anxiety on the anxiety thermometer scale**	
C	**Concentrate** Inhale deeply through your nose to the count of 4. Hold for the count of 9 Exhale through your mouth to the count of 8	Breathing Breathing changes in the brain override anxiety and stress
A	**Action** Tap on your collarbone point as you become aware of anxiety triggers. Focus on feelings that arise	E.F.T. Tapping Tapping on the collarbone is designed to calm and reduce anxiety.
L	**Listening** Listen to your anxious thoughts. Implement the "Thought-Stopping Technique" by shouting "STOP" at the negative voices and "Get Lost"	Thought -Stopping Thought-stopping diverts your attention from damaging repetitive thought habits
M	**Motivation** Visualize a calming anchor image and positive thoughts related to the situation. Imagine stepping into the image and feeling the calmness sweeping over you	Visualization Example: " I will be totally calm when making this presentation"
Assess	Hop back to your anxiety scale. If it's not at 0, repeat the "C.A.L.M. Your Alarm Technique"	

Success Story:

I had a client who came to see me, Sarah, a 38-year-old manager for a marketing company. During work meetings, her anxiety often spiraled out of control due to stress. She would worry about what her fellow peers thought of her, which often caused sleepless nights and exhaustion.

After learning the "C.A.L.M. Your Alarm Technique," Sarah decided to give it a try when she had to make an important presentation, which she had always struggled with, and her anxiety would hit the roof. On this day, her heart was racing, so she rated her anxiety on the anxiety thermometer scale, and it was a 9 out of 10.

Sarah started with the "Concentrate" step. Taking slow, deep breaths for the count of 4, holding for 8, and exhaling for 8. This helped to slow her heart rate.

Then she took "Action" and began tapping on her collarbone point as the fear of people judging her triggered her. She began tapping, focusing on her feelings as the tension started to subside.

Sarah began "Listening" to her anxious thoughts, telling her she would forget what she needed to say. Using the "Thought-Stopping Technique," she told the anxious voice to "STOP" and "Get Lost." The influence of this easy act surprised her.

To "Motivate" herself, she visualized herself confidently speaking clearly and precisely to the group.

She then hopped back to her anxiety thermometer scale, and her anxiety had reduced to a 3. Sarah successfully controlled her anxiety, delivered the presentation with a newfound calmness, and received applause from her colleagues.

To help you focus on benefiting using the "C.A.L.M. Your Alarm Technique," complete the C.A.L.M. Your Alarm Technique Tracker table. For each entry in the table include:

- **Date and Time:** Record when you used the "C.A.L.M. Your alarm Technique."
- **Situation:** Describe the specific situation or trigger that reminded you to use the technique.
- **Feelings Before:** Describe how you felt before applying the technique.
- **Feelings After:** Write down how you felt after implementing the technique.
- **Anxiety Scale:** Rate where you were before and after practicing the technique.

The "C.A.L.M. Your Alarm Technique" Tracker Table:

Date & Time	Situation	Feelings Before	Feelings After	Anxiety Scale Before	Anxiety Scale After
Date and time	Worrying about a stressful work meeting	Anxious, overwhelmed	More in control	9	4

This structured "C.A.L.M. Your Alarm Technique" Tracker Table will help you to manage your anxiety and help you develop:

- **Self-Awareness:** It helps you become more aware of your anxiety levels in different situations. Tracking the scale of anxiety before and after using specific techniques allows you to recognize your triggers and patterns.
- **Progress Monitoring:** The table will help you to monitor your progress with your anxiety. You will be able to see your anxiety levels decreasing over time and identify areas where you may need to focus.
- **Motivation:** Seeing your progress, even if only gradually, can motivate you to continue practicing this technique.

"You are never too old to set another goal or to dream a new dream" - C.S. Lewis

GOAL SETTING: THE IMPORTANCE OF SETTING YOUR GOALS TO PROPEL YOU INTO YOUR POSITIVE, CALMER FUTURE

Why is it important to set goals?

Purpose and direction: Setting clear and specific goals provides you with a sense of clarity and purpose. Your goals will give you something concrete to focus on. Creating a roadmap with each small step towards your goal will empower you, boost your self-esteem AND reduce anxiety.

Motivation and Progress Tracking: Goals act as motivators by breaking down the big picture into smaller manageable steps, making progress more achievable. Working towards your goals and progressing will boost your confidence and reduce anxiety. Providing a way to measure your progress is fundamental in managing anxiety as it gives a sense of control over your life.

Reduces Anxiety through Distraction: If you want a healthy distraction from your anxiety, set yourself goals. If you are focused on your goals, you are less likely to chew on anxious thoughts.

Why use your imagination and visualization to create an anxiety-free life?

Dream like you mean it: Imagine an anxiety-free life is like daydreaming with a purpose. Imagine if anxiety didn't hold you back. What would life be like? Picture all the fantastic places you could go and what you could do.

Goal Discovery: Using your imagination or daydreaming helps you determine what you want. If you don't have a goal, you don't know what you are aiming for.

Turning your Dreams into reality. Visualizing an anxiety-free life naturally leads to goal setting, where you can transform your dreams into specific, actionable steps. Giving you not only purpose but a clear path to follow. Reducing your anxiety by giving you back the feeling of control and moving forward.

Goals give you mind control: Your goals will highlight where you are now to your conscious and unconscious mind, creating dissatisfaction in your brain and giving you the power to drive your motivation to change your life.

Steps to setting goals:

Start small and specific: Look at your end goal and then break this down into small, realistic, and manageable steps. If your goal is to change a pattern in your life by the end of the month, take this and break it down further into weeks, days, or even hours. You will then feel more positive about what you have achieved.

Imagine standing on one side of a shallow river, and your goal is to reach the other side with stepping stones. It is necessary to slowly, methodically take one step at a time to reach the other side. With each stepping stone achieved, celebrate. You are one step closer to feeling calmer in your life.

Write it down: You're going to use your old skill in writing, which is something many of us don't do anymore.

Steer clear of jumping on your computer and typing them. Studies show you're accessing your brain's left and right hemispheres by writing down your goals. You're opening up the unconscious mind to seeing opportunities that can't be detected if you're just typing them while thinking about them. By literally writing down your goals, it transforms your thoughts into reality.

Regularly Review and Adjust: Change your goals if you need to. They are not set in stone. It is essential to review your goals often. Especially when dealing with anxiety. Some days might be trickier than others. And that's okay. If you have set a goal to go to a social event calm and relaxed and haven't quite gotten there yet, change your goal to 'I will go to the social event for at least 15 minutes and practice my relaxation techniques." Be kind to yourself.

Make your goals achievable: Many people set unrealistic goals that they cannot achieve. Of course, this creates many negative thoughts and feelings about themselves, which could trigger anxiety to flare up; obviously, this is something we want to avoid. So make them as realistic as possible to give you that motivation.

Use Positive Language: Use positive words when writing your goals. Say you had created a goal for the week: "My goal for the week is: I mustn't feel anxious when making my presentation."Word your goals in the positive.

Word your goals in the positive. So, positively wording your goals is essential. Therefore, with this example, your unconscious mind doesn't hear the word "mustn't." Thus, in effect, you're saying your goal is that you must feel anxious when making your presentation! Instead, you could say: "My goal for the week is: I am taking steps to learn how to focus on feeling calm and relaxed when making my presentation." Although they both virtually mean the same thing, our unconscious mind reads them entirely differently.

Other words to avoid are: **Can't, won't, don't, not, and never**

Complete The Goal Setting Table:

Goal	Description	Why It's Important	Specific Actions	Completion Date
Goal Example	Learn and practice stress management techniques like "the breathe not seeth technique"	By reducing my stress, it can decrease my anxiety	Practice 10 minutes of Mindfulness for seven days. Practice the "Breathe Not Seeth Technique" five times per day. Keep a stress journal	(Set a deadline)
Goal 1				
Goal 2				
Goal 3				
Goal 4				
Goal 5				

"Anxiety does not empty tomorrow of its sorrows, but only empties today of its strength" - Charles Spurgeon

Anxiety Management Technique time

Now you have your list of what you need to change and do differently to keep yourself motivated and focused. To also help you, below is a list of all the incredible techniques you've learned in the book.

Create your practice plan and work your way through these daily by listing:

- Which techniques help change the way you feel or really fire up that motivation and
- The changes you need to make as you move forward in working with your anxiety.

Then, keep practicing these on a never-ending loop in this Technique Tracker table.

The Anxiety Management Technique Tracker Table:

HACKSTER	TECHNIQUE NUMBER	TECHNIQUES	LEARNED ✓	CHECK WHICH ONES YOU'RE GOING TO BEGIN TO USE AND THEN LIST WHAT SPECIFIC ISSUE YOU ARE GOING TO WORK ON
1	1st TECHNIQUE:	THE "CALM NEW YOU TECHNIQUE"		
2	2nd TECHNIQUE:	The "BREATHE, NOT SEETHE TECHNIQUE"		
2	3rd TECHNIQUE:	The "FOR YOUR EYES ONLY TECHNIQUE"		
3	4th TECHNIQUE:	The "SHRINK & BLINK TECHNIQUE"		
3	5th TECHNIQUE:	The "INSTANT TRIGGER CHANGE TECHNIQUE"		
3	6th TECHNIQUE:	The "THOUGHT- STOPPING TECHNIQUE"		
4	7th TECHNIQUE:	"MINDFULNESS"		
4	8th TECHNIQUE:	The "EMOTION SURFING TECHNIQUE"		
5	9th TECHNIQUE:	The "SPIN AND WIN TECHNIQUE"		
5	10th TECHNIQUE:	The "EMOTIONAL FREEDOM TECHNIQUE"		
6	11th TECHNIQUE:	The "SHATTER THAT HABIT TECHNIQUE"		
6	12th TECHNIQUE:	"AFFIRMATIONS"		
7	13th TECHNIQUE:	The "C.A.L.M. YOUR ALARM TECHNIQUE"		
7	14th TECHNIQUE:	The "MOTIVATION BOOSTER TECHNIQUE"		

"Every morning brings new potential, but only if you direct the focus" - Terri Guillemets

YOUR Personalised ANXIETY ACTION PLAN

Overcoming your anxiety is about gaining knowledge and understanding about YOU and creating a customized Anxiety Action Plan. This is so exciting; your pathway through your positive changes will bring many new revelations daily. You may even find you like some of them you never knew you had tucked away in your bottom drawers.

You, too, can change. . . now

Many of my clients who have overcome anxiety say they can't quite believe they are now living a calm life; they don't have the old triggers and patterns that once would ignite their anxiety. They've changed in so many other ways. Here's how you will, too:

- **Brain Changes:** Your brain chemistry will change and create new positive neural pathways in your brain,
- **Freedom:** You'll do or go where you wish without feeling anxious,
- **End of Anxiety About Anxiety:** You'll no longer feel anxious about being anxious.

This may seem impossible to you right now, but this can and will happen to you once you make the decision now to change and follow each Hackster to overcome your anxiety.

Create Your Personalised Action Plan

It's time to incorporate all the advice, guidance, and learning you've read and create your very own action plan.

Look at the anxiety action plan example table for ideas to help you move forward, and then create your own action plan by completing the Anxiety Action Plan Table:

Anxiety Action Plan Example:

NEED TO CHANGE	DO DIFFERENTLY	FIRST STEP TO CHANGE
Manage Social Anxiety	Push yourself to go to social events with a friend	Find a local event to attend
Reduce work stress	Practice mindfulness daily	Set aside 10 minutes a day to practice mindfulness
Reduce generalized anxiety	Start to keep a daily journal to track thoughts, feelings and triggers	Buy a journal and write in it daily
Manage financial anxiety	Create a budget and consult with a financial advisor	Begin tracking your expenses for the next month
Work with family-related stress	Organize regular family meetings for open communication	Organize a family meeting for next week
Improve sleep patterns	Create a bedtime routine and limit screen time before bed	Switch off screens 1 hour before bedtime and find a good book
Minimize health Anxiety	Eat a balanced diet and begin exercising regularly	Find an exercise you enjoy. Create a weekly routine
Reduce social media stress	Set screentime limits and organize social media detox days	Decide on a social media detox day this weekend
Reduce relationship stress	Attend couples therapy or create times for open communication	Talk with your partner about when to organize a time to talk
Deal with email overload	Set specific times for checking messages	Schedule specific times for checking messages

Anxiety Action Plan Table:

NEED TO CHANGE	DO DIFFERENTLY	FIRST STEP TO CHANGE

Motivation

Imagine that you're on a journey. Your journey towards a life free from the chains of anxiety, where every day you are filled with tranquility, calmness and courage. Of course, this journey isn't always a leisurely stroll in the woods. There are winding roads and steep hills. Moments when you want to turn and run the opposite way. Times when it feels like you're trapped in an endless storm.

How often have you found yourself standing at the crossroads?

How often have you:

- Tried to stop your anxious, negative thinking patterns, and maybe it works for a time, only to end up giving in and falling back into the pattern or
- Wish you had the motivation to continue making positive changes to your habits or challenging behaviors but gave up?

To be honest, we all have moments when we feel like throwing the rag in (if you had a rag!) Changing ingrained habits or struggling with familiar fears seems impossible when it all becomes too much. And that's where motivation enters the scene as our trusty companion.

Why is motivation so important?

It's the driving force of your journey. It keeps us moving forward when the path ahead becomes too steep. Or you're the fog becomes so thick and the path ahead is a blur.

What I am going to teach you is the wonder of motivation. We will uncover the secrets to maintaining it no matter what obstacles you face. Your pathway to a calmer, anxiety-free life can be as exciting as it is challenging, and the golden key is to stay motivated with each step you take. So, if you ever need an extra push to continue moving forward on this path to anxiety reduction, this is the empowering technique you need to get yourself fired up and ready to move on to the next step.

Trust me—it works and is a fantastic tool to have right at your fingertips whenever you aren't confident about all the incredible changes you're making. So, let's learn how to instantaneously harness the extraordinary power of motivation.

Think about what motivates you explicitly to keep your focus clear. Imagine you're a volcano, and that motivation keeps erupting repeatedly to keep you moving forward.

TECHNIQUE: HOW TO WIND UP YOUR MOTIVATION WITH THE "MOTIVATION BOOSTER TECHNIQUE"

In Hackster 5, you learned the exceptional "Spin and Win Technique" skill to reduce your anxious bundle of complicated feelings. So many of my clients find that technique extremely helpful in reducing their anxiety instantly.

Please read the steps first to understand clearly what you need to do.

We're going to do something similar here to wind up your motivation as if it were an old-fashioned spinning top that you spin by pumping the handle on the top, and the longer you pump, the faster it spins. This will be you pumping up your motivation to get you to move forward.

Step	Description of the Step
1.	**Visulize your Movitavtion.** Imagine something that you're really motivated to do. It could be going on your idyllic vacation or signing the paperwork to buy your dream home. Using your imagination, visualize the scene, seeing it through your own eyes as though it's here and now. Imagine what you would see, hear, and feel. Once you have that motivation, spin this feeling inside you to intensify it.
2.	**Addressing Anxiety Pathways:** Next, imagine yourself addressing all of the different pathways connected to your anxiety, step by step, and see yourself doing so well, feeling relaxed and in control of any situation. Again, visualize the scene, imagining what you would see, hear and feel.
3.	**Intensifying Calmness:** Spin the feeling of motivation faster and faster as you think about feeling so calm in any situation.
4.	**Celebrate your Success:** Again, imagine taking your next step to overcome your anxiety, seeing and feeling how calm, proud, and delighted you are with yourself, and spin that feeling.
5.	**Continuing Progress:** Think about your next step again and follow through, feeling at ease and calm, feeling incredible motivation, and spinning that faster and faster.

Keep spinning for as long as you wish, and every time you aren't feeling motivated to go forward in life, rerun this technique to wind you up like that spinning top (Bandler, 2010).

To download copies of the tables and see bonus videos of me demonstrating each technique, sign up for the Bonus Companion Course at: https://anxietyhacks.info/info-step1/

Client Success Story:

Okay, so picture this journey of life. It's not a lazy Sunday stroll but a dynamic trek filled with hills and storms. Have you ever found yourself at a crossroads, battling negative thoughts or struggling to stay motivated for positive change? We've all been there, right?

Now, motivation is your trusty companion on this journey. It's the fuel that keeps your engine running when the road gets steep or foggy.

Meet Lily, a spirited 20-year-old trying to figure out life's twists and turns. She has found herself at a crossroads, wrestling with anxiety and negative whispers and struggling to stay committed to positive change. Enter the "Motivation Booster Technique," a life-changing tool for Lily's toolbox to break her anxiety patterns.

Lily's Crossroads:

Lily faced those moments we all know – the battle between wanting to silence anxious thoughts and the fleeting motivation to make positive shits. Life's challenges felt like steep hills and foggy uncertainties often obscured the path forward.

The Motivation Booster Unveiled:

Lily dove into the Motivation Booster Technique, and it became her beacon on stormy nights, a tool to keep the flame of determination burning bright.

Lily's journey through the technique:

Visualizing Dreams: Lily imaged her dream vacation, seeing crystal clear scenes of relaxation. As she spun this vision, her motivation surged.

Conquering Anxiety Pathways: She visualized herself mastering each step in the face of anxiety, and Lily took charge. She pained a vivid picture of success, step by step.

Intensifying Calmness: the feeling of calmness becomes her armor. Lily spun this emotion faster, embracing tranquility in the face of life's storms.

Celebrating Success: in her mind's eye, Lily reveled in success – calm, proud and delighted. With each mental celebration, she spun the motivation faster.

#**Continued Progress:** Lily visualized her next steps, feeling incredibly motivated. With each imagined stride, the spinning accelerated.

The transformation Unleased:

The Motivation Booster Technique wasn't just a one-time wonder for Lily. It became her main tool in every motivational path. Whether facing a daunting task or feeling unsure, Lily would rerun the technique, reigniting her inner fire.

So Lily's journey isn't just about tackling anxiety: it's about conquering each challenge with a newfound motivation. The once daunting hills become exciting climbs, and the fog is lifted to reveal a path filled with exciting possibilities.

So, if Lily can turn her motivation into a superpower, so can you. Let's roll forward with motivation as our guide!

"The mind is everything. What you think you become" – Buddha

Therapies for Overcoming Anxiety

A wide variety of therapies can help you, but it's all about finding the right one that works for you. Treatment for anxiety is most effective when it focuses on various areas like:

- Past events that could have triggered or influenced your anxiety,
- Depression, anger, and failure,
- Reducing the stresses of life that increase your anxiety,
- Exploring the connection between emotions and anxiety and
- The causes of your behaviors.

A multi-directional approach is often best when treating anxiety.

Suggestions for therapies that could help you:

Therapy	**Description**
Psychotherapy	Psychotherapy, a talking therapy, involves a trained therapist helping to explore thoughts, emotions and behaviors in a safe and confidential setting. Assist in developing coping strategies and gain insight into the root causes of anxiety
Cognitive-behavioral therapy (C.B.T.)	C.B.T. focuses on identifying and changing negative thought patterns and behaviors
Hypnotherapy	Hypnotherapy is a guided process that uses relaxation to help access the subconscious mind and explore negative behavior patterns, promoting relaxation, reducing anxiety and addressing the root causes of anxiety
Neuro-Linguistic Programming (N.L.P.)	N.L.P. is a method that helps reframe thinking and change unhelpful behaviors, providing practical techniques to manage anxiety
Mindfulness	Mindfulness is a meditation-based approach that guides people to focus on the present moment with judgment, promotion relation, reducing stress and anxiety
Exposure Therapy	Exposure therapy involves gradual and controlled exposure to anxiety-inducing situations, guiding you to become less fearful over time
Eye Movement Desensitization and Reprocessing (E.M.D.R.)	E.M.D.R. is mainly used for trauma-related anxiety, which can reduce the emotional impact of traumatic memories, alleviating feelings of anxiety
Group Therapy	Group therapy involves a group of people with similar concerns discussing and supporting each other

For support and guidance, research the many therapies out there and find the right one for you.

EXTRA TOOLS FOR YOUR TOOLBOX TO A CALMER YOU

In this Hackster, you have learned a wealth of valuable insights and techniques focused on moving forward in reducing your anxiety as you work through this workbook.

The key takeaways you have learned are:

The "C.A.L.M. Your Alarm Technique:"

- The "C.A.L.M. Your Alarm Technique" acronym guides you through specific techniques: Concentration, Action, Listen and Motivation. This is just what you need to help you move forward in reducing your anxiety.
- With so many benefits, of course, reducing your anxiety but also stress levels, improving your sleep patterns and increasing self-confidence, what more do you need so hop in and learn this technique with your deep breathing, E.F.T. tapping, thought stopping and motivation visualization, you can do it.

Goal Setting:

- Taking your big goal and turning it into smaller steps will act as motivation, and creating clear, specific goals will also motivate you to provide purpose and clarity, measure your progress and reduce anxiety through distraction.
- Your steps to set successful goals: create specific and small goals, write them down, regularly check over and adjust them as you make them achievable with positive language.

Technique Time

- Maintain a list of the techniques you have learned throughout the workbook.
- Create your own practice plan by choosing which technique you feel will be the most beneficial in managing your anxiety effectively or boosting your motivation.
- It also helps you plan how to incorporate them into your daily routine for consistent practice.

Your Personalised Anxiety Action Plan:

- Overcoming anxiety involves gaining knowledge about your patterns of behavior connected to your anxiety and understanding of yourself.
- Create an Anxiety Action Plan that includes a list of what you need to change and what you will begin to do differently.
- Work on one change at a time and celebrate your progress.

The Motivation Booster Technique:

- Motivation is the driving force that keeps you moving forward in combatting your anxiety.
- The "Motivation Booster Technique" will help you maintain your motivation during challenging times.
- Visualize something that motivates you, addresses anxiety pathways, intensifies feelings of calmness and motivation and keeps that motivation spinning.

"Feelings come and go like clouds in a windy sky. Conscious breathing is my anchor" - Thich Nhat Hanh

Review and Reflection:

Answer these questions to help you understand what you have learned in this Hackster and how you can use it to create a calmer you:

1. **The "C.A.L.M. Your Alarm Technique:"**
   What strategies or techniques have you found most effective in reducing your anxiety levels, and how consistently have you been using them?

   Explain a specific instance when you successfully used the "C.A.L.M. Your Alarm Technique" to regain control over your anxiety and what the result was.

   ---

2. Goal Setting:
   What are three long-term goals you believe can significantly improve your well-being and help reduce your anxiety?

   Why do you believe these goals are essential?

How do you currently track your progress in reaching your goals? Which strategies or techniques do you use to stay motivated and on track?

____

____

3. Technique Time:

Which anxiety management techniques from the workbook resonate with you the most, and how will you implement them into your daily routine to keep you focused on changing your patterns?

____

____

Describe a situation when you applied one of the techniques from the workbook to manage your anxiety effectively.

____

____

How did it make you feel?

____

____

4. Your Personalised Anxiety Action Plan:

1. After completing your anxiety action plan, which changes do you think will most benefit your anxiety reduction?

____

____

2. How do you plan to apply these changes?

____

____

The "Motivation Booster Technique:"

Describe the physical and emotional sensations you experience while using the "Motivation Booster Technique."

Write down three specific situations in your life where the "Motivation Booster Technique" would be most beneficial.

Hackster 7: And Finally:

As we reach the finale of this transformative pathway in Hackster 7, you've acquired insights and a powerful toolkit to manage anxiety effectively. It's a moment to revel in your progress, a testament to your resilience and commitment. Now, armed with the "C.A.L.M. Your Alarm Technique," you stand at the threshold of newfound calmness and control.

Remember, this journey is about more than conquering anxiety. It's a testament to your strength and determination. The path ahead may hold challenges, but each step forward is a victory. Keep moving, keep growing, and embrace the unwavering power within you to sculpt a life free from the clutches of anxiety. Your journey doesn't end here. It evolves into a lifelong commitment to your well-being and a future filled with tranquility.

"Bravery is the compass that points you away from anxiety and toward a life of relaxation and strength" – Kate Hudson-Hall

Thriving Beyond Anxiety: Your Ongoing Journey

Congratulations on completing the Anxiety Hacks Workbook! Your journey to conquer anxiety has just taken a significant step forward. Here's your guide for what comes next:

Stay Focused and Experiment: Continue experimenting with the diverse techniques you've learned. Each trial is a step toward understanding and overcoming your anxiety.

Complete the Tables: Take the time to fill in the tables associated with each technique. These are valuable tools designed to help you unravel your anxiety triggers, behaviors and patterns.

Goal Setting: Set clear and achievable goals for yourself. Outline small, actionable steps that align with your journey to a calmer you.

Reach Out to Me: Please reach out if you need guidance or share your progress. I love hearing from my readers and am committed to responding to every message.

Thank you for joining me on this adventure towards a life free from the shackles of anxiety. Your commitment to growth and self-discovery is truly admirable. Remember, I'm here to support you every step of the way. Keep changing.

REFERENCES

Bandler, R. (2010). Get The Life You Want. HarperElement

Bandler, R., Roberti, A, & Fitzpatrick, O. (2013). The Ultimate Introduction To NLP: How to Build A Successful Life. HarperCollins

Craig, G., & Craig, T. (n.d.). "How to do the EFT tapping basics - The basic recipe." https://www.emofree.com/nl/eft-tutorial/ tapping-basics/how-to-do-eft.html

NEED MORE HELP THROUGH YOUR POSITIVE CHANGES?

How to contact me:

Yes, I'd love to connect. I so enjoy helping people to change their behaviors and reduce anxiety. Find me at:

Website: katehudson-hall.com

Email: katehudsonhall@gmail.com

For my books and social media links: https://linktr.ee/katehudsonhall

THERAPY: I see clients one-to-one, either in person or online, via Zoom, WhatsApp, Facetime, and other web-based services.

"SMALL STEPS IN THE RIGHT DIRECTION CAN TURN OUT TO BE THE BIGGEST STEP OF YOUR LIFE" — Anonymous

ACKNOWLEDGMENTS

I would like to dedicate this book to all the incredible people who have inspired me to write this book, especially:

Alan, whose incredible encouragement and belief in me never wavers.

My three-and-a-half musketeers, Luca, Tino and Pads, plus my dazzling, funny, and creative granddaughter, Lila, for being the comedic backbone of my life. Also, thank you for graciously providing an ear when I need to waffle, although I'm not entirely convinced any of you are truly tuned in!

Best-selling author, Leslie Lindsey Davis, the formatting-5-star, Very Reverend Angel! With a wave of your mouse, and a finger to point, you made formatting nightmares disappear faster than Inspector Featherstone Flapsworth in a pet shop. THANK YOU.

Lassie, Rover, Winston and Petunia
and their never-ending unconditional love and poops!

Those with anxiety.
Stay focused on your pathway to calmness because you CAN achieve this.

THE FREE ANXIETY HACKS BONUS COMPANION COURSE

Unlock a richer journey to conquer anxiety with the FREE Anxiety Hacks Bonus Companion Course. Join me now for an immersive experience:

- **Gain access to enlightening bonus video demonstrations for every technique.**
- **Enjoy exclusive content and valuable resources to amplify your progress.**
- **Dive into downloadable worksheets and templates tailored to each Hackster.**

Step into the next chapter of your anxiety-free life –
Sign up today and empower yourself for lasting positive change!

See you on the other side!

Visit the following link to get free access to your bonus materials now:

https://anxietyhacks.info/info-step1/

ABOUT KATE HUDSON-HALL

At the age of five, Kate began her anxiety career in earnest. Thirty years later, and after much help, she eventually freed herself from the weighty clutches of anxiety (although it has popped up now and again, she had learned the tools to deal with this beast!). Kate then stepped out and decided to take a different anxiety pathway. Feeling the great need to help others as she had been helped, she trained as a psychotherapist, hypnotherapist and NLP practitioner, among other therapies.

Having spent the last two decades working as an anxiety therapist and wanting to reach out further than just her immediate clientele, Kate decided to write this book, pouring into it all she has learned and experienced in helping others with anxiety.

Kate lives and works in London and occasionally escapes to spend summers enjoying the views from the middle of a field on her land in Cornwall, overlooking the Atlantic Ocean.

Kate once spoke to the Queen on the telephone, by accident, who wanted to know if she was "The General Public". . . she had to come clean. . . and admit it!

OTHER BOOKS BY KATE HUDSON-HALL

For more information and to find the link for each book, visit https://linktr.ee/katehudsonhallbooks

Anxiety Hacks Proven Techniques, Tools and Tips to Calmness

Anxiety Hacks Proven Techniques, Tools and Tips to Calmness. (The audiobook)

Anxiety Hacks Journal: Your Daily Practice for Anxiety Relief

Bulimia Sucks! 10 Steps to Break Bingeing & Purging Patterns

Bulimia Sucks! 10 Steps to Break Bingeing & Purging Patterns. (The audiobook)

Bulimia Sucks! Personal Workbook Bulimia Sucks! Personal Food Journal

Coloring Book Series:

Anxiety Relief Anorexia Sucks!

Bulimia Sucks!

Binge Eating Sucks!

Drawing by Mildred Rose

REVIEW REQUEST

CAN YOU HELP?

Thank You for Reading My Book. I do hope it is helping reduce your anxiety levels.

I really appreciate all your feedback, and I love hearing your thoughts.

So, I need your input to make this book's next version and future books even more empowering.

Please leave me an honest review on Amazon; I would love to know what you thought of the book.

Thank you so much!

Kate Hudson-Hall

Printed in Great Britain
by Amazon

39516899R00117